The Church School

THE ORGANIZATION, ADMINISTRATION, AND
SUPERVISION OF CHRISTIAN EDUCATION
IN THE LOCAL CHURCH

By Paul H. Vieth

THIS is a comprehensive guide for church school superintendents, principals of departments, committees on Christian education, pastors, and other workers who share responsibility for developing an effective program of Christian education in the local church. The author writes simply and concisely, in language that laymen can readily understand. His chief emphasis is on good practice, but his counsel is supported by illuminating statements of theory.

Such subjects as "The Church and Christian Education," "The Curriculum of Christian Education," "The Curriculum of Worship," "Improving Teaching," "Awards and Discipline," "The Training of Workers," and "Church School and Home" are treated with the wisdom and skill for which Dr. Vieth is known both at home and abroad. His book comes out of the experience of one who has spent 40 years of his life in Christian education.

Workers in every type of church school, large or small, rural or urban, rich or poor, will find here a thoughtful, realistic, and sympathetic consideration of their tasks and their problems, and clear directions for imaginative, hopeful action. A serious use of the book would lift their schools to new levels of effectiveness.

THE CHURCH SCHOOL

Paul H. Vieth

The Church School

The Organization, Administration,
and Supervision of Christian
Education in the Local Church

CHRISTIAN EDUCATION PRESS
PHILADELPHIA PENNSYLVANIA

Copyright 1957
The Christian Education Press

SECOND PRINTING, 1958
THIRD PRINTING, 1960
FOURTH PRINTING, 1963

Library of Congress Catalog Card Number: 57-14607

TABLE OF CONTENTS

1 WHY THIS BOOK?

A church school superintendent writes: "I have been appointed superintendent of my church school. I am a public school teacher, but my experience in church school work is negative. This is an enormous task and your help will be most welcome." Another writes: "Please give me some suggestions on how I can become a better superintendent."

This appeal for help could be multiplied a thousand fold. It is voiced not only by superintendents, but also by pastors, department principals, committee members, and teachers. It comes from workers with years of experience as well as from those recently appointed. It is echoed by farmers, business men, housewives, and professional men and women. All agree that conducting a church school is an enormous job.

1. *This book attempts to answer these appeals.* It is concerned with the problems of conducting church schools. It comes out of the experience of one who has spent 40 years of his life in Christian education, and has

served in church schools as teacher, department principal, superintendent, director of Christian education, and member of committees on Christian education. He has heard and sought to answer the problems of thousands of superintendents, pastors, and other officers, in conventions and institutes. In immediate preparation for this writing, he has asked the church school superintendents of several hundred churches to state their most pressing problems, to which 150 generously responded.

These superintendents preside over large church schools and small, rural and urban, rich and poor. They include both men and women. Their situations are probably representative of the more than 400,000 church schools in the Protestant churches of the world. These church schools, in vital relationship with Christian homes, are one of the church's chief means for recruitment, evangelism, nurture, and training. Many of them are far less effective than they ought to be and could be. If they can be improved, the whole Christian cause will thereby be advanced.

The modern church school had its origin outside the church. It was a layman's movement. Although the church has now adopted the church school as its own, the tradition of having chief responsibility for it in the hands of lay men and women has continued. While we shall insist that the pastor of a church must be in vital relationship with the church school, we shall assume that lay men and women are in large measure responsible for solving the problems with which we will deal. We shall respect the layman's situation which requires him to fit his church school work into a busy life as best he can. This demands that problems be clearly stated for ready reference, simply and concisely treated, in language which is not technical, and with chief emphasis on good practice, supported by theory only as necessary.

2. *What is the relation of theory and practice?* It was our original intention to write a simple manual of practical suggestions, and to avoid theoretical considerations. This proved not to be feasible. Good practice can follow only from sound theory. Laymen are justly suspicious of theory which does not result in practical applications, but the cure is not to have no theory, but to have better theory from which meaningful practice can result. It is sterile to do something a certain way without understanding why it should be done that way. Moreover, life presents many new problems which cannot be successfully met without understanding the principles which point the way to solutions. Some readers will probably say, "Too much theory!" but others may say with equal justice, "Too much detail! Why don't you get on with the job?" This is a risk we have had to take.

3. *Creative effort is necessary.* Not all the requests which were made by our correspondents could be answered in one book. We believe, however, that those who read the following chapters diligently will find reference to most of their questions either directly or by implication. What will be more disappointing is that no sure-fire solutions can be given to many problems. There are no simple five-finger exercises to meet all needs. Many problems are peculiar to the churches in which they exist, and to the people who are wrestling with them. The best we could do is to try and help you think out your own solutions. Effective church school administration requires creative effort, guided by sound principles, and a spirit of patience and love.

Workers in small church schools are likely to feel that

those who write books do not understand their problems. Perhaps the following chapters will give that impression so far as this book is concerned. Nevertheless, let us state our conviction that the small church schools are just as important as the larger ones. Some of the best Christian education is done in small churches. Many problems are easier to solve with smaller numbers. Unfortunately, a writer cannot give a complete pattern of organization for a church school without implying a complexity which makes it unrealistic for small churches. This forces the small church to make the necessary adaptations to fit its situation. Wherever possible, we have made suggestions on how these adaptations may be made.

4. *What does this book cover?* Since this book is written for those who have general responsibility for conducting church schools, it will not deal directly with the work of the teachers. It is concerned with those matters which provide the conditions for effective teaching. These may be roughly classified into the following groups:

(1) *Organization.* The church school must have a working organization. Good organization assures proper relation to the church as a whole. It is concerned with the arrangement of pupils by departments and classes, and the placement of these groups in available rooms. It provides for proper time schedules, and the prompt and orderly movement of departments and classes to and from their places of work. It arranges the working staff into an effective team, with duties and relationships clearly defined.

(2) *Administration.* Good administration is concerned with carrying policies and plans into effective action. It assures the smooth running of the organization. It provides curriculum and resource materials and sees that they

4

are readily available to workers. It is concerned with the enlistment of capable workers, and providing classes and conferences for their training. It plans for the enrollment of new pupils and their proper placement in classes, the keeping of adequate records, the follow-up of absentees, and annual promotions. It is concerned with the most effective use of rooms and equipment, and with providing better equipment when needed. It makes the best use of special days and occasions. It develops working relations with the homes.

(3) *Supervision.* This includes all those activities which are concerned with the improvement of the church school so that it may do its work more effectively. It establishes high standards and seeks to attain them. Good supervision seeks to get the whole church to take greater responsibility for the church school. It is concerned with maintaining good order and developing a high morale. It aims at improving the effectiveness of workers by fostering unity in a common purpose, and training them for better work through group meetings, training classes, and personal guidance.

It is not entirely correct to say that these activities are distinguished from teaching. In a broad sense, they are educational in nature. The general attitude of the church, the spirit of the church school, the first contacts of the church with pupils and their parents, the interest and enthusiasm of teachers—all these are effective elements in what pupils learn in the church school. Moreover, in their guidance of other workers, general officers are engaged in teaching in the highest sense of the term.

Organization, administration, and supervision are general terms which describe the duties of those who are responsible for conducting church schools. The questions asked by our correspondents are much more specific. They are concerned with such problems as these:

How should the church school be related to the church? What type of organization best expresses this relationship? How should pupils be grouped in departments and classes? What is the best plan of financing the church school? In these matters, how do small church schools differ from large?

What are the duties of a superintendent? the pastor? other officers? How are these officers related to each other, and how can they best work together?

What lesson materials and other resources should be used? How can teaching be made more interesting? How can we know when our teaching is effective? How can we get good order? What should be the nature of worship programs in the different departments? Should there be an assembly for the whole church school? What shall we do in the small school which cannot have separate departments? Who should lead the worship services? Where can we find prayers and other materials suitable for worship?

How can we get parents to take an interest in the church school? How can we get parents to attend church school? What kind of parent-teacher meetings should we have? How can we get parents to co-operate in having pupils do their home assignments?

How can we increase our attendance? Is it feasible to run church school buses? How can we hold post-confirmation young people? How can we get adults to come into the church school? How can we get pupils and teachers to come on time, and regularly? What kinds of records are important?

What kind of equipment is best? What can we do when

6

we are over-crowded? Are separate classrooms necessary? By what plans can we use rooms and equipment more than once per Sunday?

5. *How to Use This Book.* One way to use a book is to read it from beginning to end. If it is your own copy, you can take your pencil and mark the parts to which you want to return later. We suspect, however, that many busy readers will want help on specific problems when there is no time to read an entire book. For their convenience we have done two things: (1) liberally sprinkled each chapter with sub-division headings, side headings, numbered paragraphs, and questions. Thus many topics can be readily located by scanning through the pages of the appropriate chapter; (2) included a final chapter of problems classified under appropriate headings, with page numbers where they are treated. This is in place of the customary topical index.

6. *Some other books are recommended.* There are many excellent books in which some of the subjects on which we touch are more fully treated. We shall not burden the reader with reference to many of these, since most of them will not be available to him. There are, however, a few which are so useful that references to them will occur in a number of places. It is recommended that these be purchased. They will make a good addition to the workers' library. They include the following:

A Guide for Curriculum in Christian Education, National Council of Churches, New York, 1955. $2.25.

Foster, Virgil E., *How a Small Church Can Have Good Christian Education.* Harper & Brothers, 1956. $2.00.

Lobingier, J. L., *If Teaching Is Your Job*. The Pilgrim Press, 1956. $2.50.

Lobingier, J. L., *The Better Church School*. The Pilgrim Press, 1952. $2.00.

Paulsen, I. G., *The Church School and Worship*. Abingdon Press, 1940. $1.00.

2 THE CHURCH AND CHRISTIAN EDUCATION

Organization and program for Christian education must be understood and planned in light of the nature and purpose of the church. The church school is created by the church. It has no independent life of its own. It exists only within the total life and work of the church. It is maintained in obedience to Christ's command "Go therefore . . . *teaching* them to observe all things I have commanded you" (Matt. 28:19-20).

WHAT IS THE CHURCH?

Perhaps no one who reads these pages has not been aware of and acquainted with the church from childhood. Yet few can give any satisfactory statement of just what is the church. Even the greatest theologians who have sought to define the church find themselves in disagreement. In its fullness of meaning and significance, the church is too great to be confined in the words of a defi-

9

nition. The best we can do is to give our own confession of faith concerning what the church means to us.

The church is a divine-human agency, created by God, through Christ who is its Head, and indwelt by his Holy Spirit. It consists of people who have responded to God's love and seek to do his will.

The visible church is not a building which is popularly called "church." Important as the building may be for its activities, a church can exist without a building, and even the most magnificent building does not make a church. The church is people. But not just any group of people make a church.

The church is people in relation to God. They acknowledge their dependence on God for his providence and grace, and respond to him in love and obedience to his will. They hold in common a faith in Jesus Christ as their Savior, Lord, and Teacher. They take joy in the common worship of God.

The church is people in special relation with each other. Individuals in solitary relation to God do not constitute a church. God's people are a congregation, bound to each other in Christian fellowship. The ties that bind them together are their common faith in God through Jesus Christ, love of one another such as Paul describes in 1 Corinthians 13, and the desire to work together in the service of God. This Christian fellowship finds its most concrete expression in the local congregation, but it does not stop there. If the spirit of Christ is genuinely present, the fellowship includes other churches in the community and extends in ever widening circles to embrace Christians throughout the world without regard to nation or race. It is inspired also by those who have gone before in the long history of the church.

When we say that the church is a divine-human agency, we mean that it has one foot in heaven and the other on this earth. It is a community which has Christ as its Head. It is above this world and seeks only to know and to do God's will. It is a veritable "colony of heaven" (Philippians 3:20, Moffat translation). It sits in judgment on nations and societies as well as individual persons when these are disobedient to the revealed will of God. But it is also of this earth. Its members are human beings with all their ignorance, pride, sinfulness, and follies. It lives in the midst of the world and is easily influenced by the society of which it is a part, while at the same time seeking to redeem that society.

WHAT THE CHURCH DOES

The church is not an end in itself, but an instrument through which God may work his will. What, then, is the purpose of the church? To this question many answers have been given, varying with time and place and the particular theological outlook of the writers. After a review of these many answers, H. Richard Niebuhr has concluded: "Is not the result of all these debates and the content of the confessions or commandments of all these authorities this: That no substitute can be found for the definition of the goal of the church as the *increase among men of the love of God and neighbor?*"[1] We cannot do better than to accept this simple definition of the purpose of the church.

To achieve its purpose, the church must be active in Christian work. This leads to a variety of efforts which constitute its total program. To name all the things which churches do would make a long list indeed. Most of them

---

[1] Niebuhr, H. Richard, *The Purpose of the Church and Its Ministry*, p 31. Harper & Brothers.

will fall under one or more of the following headings:

1. *Worship.* The worship of God is at the heart of what any congregation is and does, as it is also central in the life of the individual Christian. Through worshiping together the congregation expresses its adoration of God, its dependence on him, and its gratitude for his love and grace. The observance of the sacraments is for many the high point of worship.

2. *Christian Fellowship.* L. J. Sherrill has described the Christian community as "a *koinonia*[2] in which both men and God participate in an intricate web of relationships. The *koinonia* exists in the household quite as truly as it does in the church. But always in *koinonia*, by virtue of its own nature, it is understood and avowed that God is participant."[3] Such a fellowship is created by the Holy Spirit and is the means through which he works among men.

This fellowship is not so much created through activities which seek to promote it, as it is a spirit which pervades and is fostered by association in love in all the work of the church. It is enhanced by methods of work through which persons are enabled to understand and accept one another, and to be most truly themselves. But there are properly also some activities of a social nature whose purpose is to help build the congregation into a fellowship.

3. *Proclamation and Teaching.* Knowledge and understanding of God's Word, the Christian faith, the church and its work, and the implications of all these for individual and social living, is a constant need of young and old.

---

[2] *Koinonia* is the New Testament Greek word for this loving relationship in the Christian community for which there is no adequate English translation.

[3] Sherrill, L. J., *The Gift of Power*, pp. 82, 83. Macmillan, 1955.

While it is customary to think of Christian teaching as being primarily for the young, it is actually a continuing need of all. Every member of the congregation stands before God in constant need of greater understanding and acceptance of what it means to be a Christian. A congregation which limits Christian education to the young will become sterile because it is denying itself a means for constant renewal and enrichment.

Some would make a distinction between preaching and teaching, thinking of preaching as the proclamation of God's Word and call to repentance, and teaching as the effort to expand and deepen the understanding of the faith in those who have already responded to God's call. Perhaps this distinction should be made. However, there is no effective Christian teaching which is not also proclamation and call, and most preaching includes also exposition and interpretation as well as proclamation. The central purpose of both preaching and teaching is evangelism— commitment and ever renewed commitment to Christian discipleship. We need the best of both preaching and teaching.

4. *Pastoral Care.* To visit the sick, help the perplexed and distressed, comfort the bereaved, and serve those in need has always been regarded as an important expression of the Christian spirit. The minister's work in personal counseling is becoming increasingly important. It is a mistake, however, to assume that all these things will be done only by the minister, in behalf of the congregation. "Bear ye one another's burdens" applies to all members of the loving Christian community.

5. *Extension.* Under this heading we may group all those activities whose purpose is to bring community, nation, and world increasingly under the rulership of Christ.

It includes evangelism to bring the call of Christ to those outside the church; missions to extend the gospel around the world as well as into every corner of the homeland; social service and social action to help bring about justice, goodwill, and brotherhood in all human relations.

6. *Administration*. To do its work, the church needs to be an effectively working body. This requires organization, budget, building, equipment, and maintenance. At first glance, these matters appear to be secondary in nature, having importance only because they make the primary work of the church possible. Actually this is not the case. The giving and spending of money, serving as officers and on committees, making the building really a proper house for God, all of these are expressions of the inner spiritual life of the members—and in turn have an effect on spiritual development.

THE NEED FOR AND DANGER OF ORGANIZATION

These activities are all the concern of the whole church. In the case of some, like public worship, the congregation acts as a whole. In others, the work is best done by officers and committees representing the congregation, and through agencies representing particular ages and interests. In many cases smaller groups than a whole congregation are necessary. Hence there is need for good organization.

In spite of the need for organization, there are also dangers. People may become so concerned with the organization that they mistake it for the purpose which it exists to serve. It must always be a means to a prior purpose, and only that organization is good which best serves the purpose for which it exists. Agencies within the church may become so self-centered and independent that members forget their primary relation and loyalty to the whole congregation. It is essential that unity of purpose and program be maintained, in spite of necessary diversity of work. In the spirit of 1 Corinthians 12, there are diversities of offices and tasks, but all are members of one body.

This unity of purpose and program, with diversity of groups and activities, may be shown by the following diagram.

Chart I

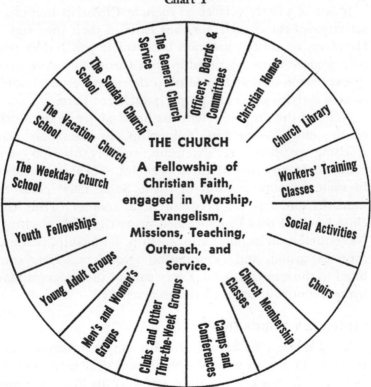

All that is within the circle constitutes the church in action, no matter by what particular name it may be called. The whole constitutes the Christian community, and no part has meaning or purpose outside that whole. The agencies named constitute the means through which the whole achieves its purpose. It could be argued that the general church worship is so central that it should not be made parallel with other agencies, but the latter has been done in this diagram to show it as an organized activity through which the church expresses its life.

It is not strictly correct to include Christian homes as activities of the church, for they exist in their own right. However, no church program is complete which does not take account of its relationship with Christian homes, and in expression of that relationship there are certain home-church activities that are properly included here.

None of the program elements listed above as the work of the church—worship, fellowship, proclamation and teaching, pastoral care, extension, and organization—are confined to any one of these agencies. They are present in some measure in most of them. Some may specialize more in one type of program than another. Thus the church school may be concerned primarily with teaching. Nevertheless, it includes also worship, fellowship, pastoral care, extension, and organization. Nor is teaching confined to the church school. Every part of the program may make a contribution to Christian teaching.

CHRISTIAN EDUCATION

To this point we have dealt with the total purpose and program of the church. We shall now deal more specifically with its work of teaching, which in its broadest sense is called Christian education.

Christian education is not an optional or second-rate interest of the church. With worship, preaching, evangelism, missions, and good works, it is at the very heart of the church's program. It is a concern of the whole congregation, and cannot be left just to those who have been given specific responsibility for carrying on the educational program.

Christian education is more than teaching *about* the Christian religion. It is education *into* the Christian life. It introduces the learner to knowledge about God, man's relation to God, the Bible, the church and the meaning of Christian living. But it does not end with giving knowledge. It seeks so to touch the learner's whole life that it may become his purpose to do the will of God. It seeks to bring every person more fully into the church, to help him find strength in its fellowship and joy in its work.

The Aim. The aim of Christian education may be summed up in the one word *discipleship*. A disciple is one who has committed his life to God through Christ and knows that he has been accepted by him. He has a living faith in God, with convictions about God's relation to the world and to men, and man's dependence on and obligation to God. He has a Christian attitude toward himself and others. He has a living hope that God's kingdom will come, and his will be done on earth as it is in heaven. He is a living witness to his Christian faith in both word and deed.[4]

If it be argued that this high purpose is not the aim of Christian education only, but of the whole church for every person in its fellowship, we are prepared to accept

---

[4] The author acknowledges indebtedness to James D. Smart for this approach to the statement of aim. See especially p. 107 in his *The Teaching Ministry of the Church.*

17

the point. It is proof of the fact that the purpose of the church is one, and that each agency must minister to that purpose. Christian education does not have aims of its own. It exists to achieve the purpose of the church.

The aims of Christian education are not achieved by imposing on immature minds a knowledge of the Bible, having them learn and repeat statements of faith, or engaging them in "religious" activities. There must be inner transformation. Discipleship involves the whole person in re-birth and commitment. Hence Christian education can develop effective practice only on the basis of an understanding of what persons are and how they learn.

2. *Nature of the Learner.* Such knowledge is based on the general study of persons and how they learn (psychology) and on the insights which come from the Christian interpretation of man (theology). Psychology emphasizes the importance of relating teaching to the pupil's interest and need. It takes account of the growing capacity to learn with increasing maturity: "When I was a child, I spoke like a child, I thought like a child, I reasoned like a child; when I became a man, I gave up childish ways" (1 Cor. 13:11). It relies on nurture and development, and seeks to keep pace with growing capacities: "First the blade, then the ear, then the full grain in the ear" (Mark 4:28). Theology views man as made in the divine image, a child of God. It is as natural for him to turn to God as for a flower to turn to the sun. But man is also a sinner, with impulses which lead him to do the things which he ought not to do, and to leave undone the things that he ought to do. He loves himself more than others and God. He needs to be saved from sin. This deliverance can come only by gratefully receiving what God has done for him through Jesus Christ and continues to do through the Holy Spirit.

What, then, can the church do through Christian education? Redemption and faith are gifts from God. But nurture in the things of the spirit which may lead to Christian faith and life is a responsibility of the home and the church, in humble dependence on God. Christian education works in the faith that God needs and uses Christian parents and teachers in his divine purpose.

HOW THE CHURCH TEACHES

There are two main ways through which the church teaches Christian discipleship. The first is indirect and unplanned; the second is planned and organized.

1. *Through Participation in Christian Fellowship.* The church teaches by what it is and does. More than a century ago, Horace Bushnell said, "You teach Christ not by words only, but by so living as to make your own life the interpreter of his." He was writing of the Christian family, and emphasized the fact that within its close relationships a power over the character of its members is exerted which is not deliberately planned or consciously taught. "We conceive the manners, personal views, prejudices, practical motives, and spirit of the house as an atmosphere which passes into all and pervades all, as naturally as the air they breathe."[5]

What Bushnell said of the family is also true of a church which is a dynamic Christian fellowship of old and young. The faith of the church, expressed in devotion to God, loyalty to Christ, and service to others, provides an atmosphere which unconsciously influences those associated with it. Children as well as older people who have a sense of belonging to this fellowship, feel its love, and share its

---

[5] Bushnell, Horace, *Christian Nurture*, pp. 76, 77. Yale University Press. Reprinted 1947.

worship and work, are thereby given a foundation in experience which is basic to Christian teaching. Participation in the church's life and work is a means to understanding its purpose and mission. He who engages in worship will learn more about the true meaning of Christian worship than he can learn from mere instruction in worship. He who serves as an officer or on a committee will thereby learn about the mission of the church and tend to accept it as his own. He who teaches the Bible to others will gain a deeper knowledge and appreciation of the Bible. He who responds to human need through gifts of service and money will learn the joy and grace of stewardship.

This experience in the Christian community is so basic to Christian education that it is to be questioned whether the aims of Christian education can be achieved without it. The church school depends on it so much for its effectiveness that those responsible for its leadership will do well to make every effort to help its members to gain a real sense of being accepted into and being a part of the whole Body of Christ. The whole congregation should be concerned with extending its spirit and fellowship to all related to it. This is especially important as it affects children, because they are most sensitive to atmosphere and yet so often ignored by the adult congregation.

This participation in Christian community comes to its fullest expression in common worship, but it is also present in other activities, and should become real through every relationship which the individual has with the church. It may be most intimately present in the smaller organized groups within the church. For younger children in particular, it is first met in their department groups where they are in association with each other and with adults who are representative of the church as a whole.

This emphasis on atmosphere and participation gives us a clue to the important place that the Christian family takes in Christian education. A Christian family is an extension of the spirit and atmosphere of the church into the home. The home provides the intimate relationships and the continuous living together which are so essential to Christian development. The concern of Christian education with home relationships cannot end with a desire for home cooperation in the work of the church school. It must first of all be for the development of Christian families which have the power to teach Christ by being themselves Christian.

2. *Through Maintaining a Church School.* The church teaches through an organized educational program. Although the experience of belonging to and participating in the Christian community is basic, Christian education requires more than this. Take an example from public education. Although his experience in his family and community are basic to the education of the child, the community provides a school in which many things must be taught that do not result from mere living in the community. Basic skills must be learned, a vast background of knowledge must be acquired, community life must be interpreted, acceptable patterns of life in a democracy must be established, principles and ideals of living must be imparted. This is also true for Christian education. A vast amount of teaching must be done if persons are to understand and accept the Christian faith and give expression to it in Christian life. This requires classes and other learning groups, time schedules, rooms and equipment, curriculum, teachers, and other factors which make an effective teaching and learning situation. This is Chris-

tian education in the usual sense of the word. For this the church has a church school.

SUMMARY OF PRINCIPLES

We have considered the nature of the church and the place of Christian education in its purpose and program. From this there emerge certain principles which will underlie all that follows in subsequent chapters. These are summarized in the following propositions:

1. Christian education is one of the basic means through which the church seeks to accomplish its mission of increasing among men the love of God and neighbor.

2. Christian education is wholly included within the purpose and program of the church, and never independent from them.

3. Christian education is of equal importance with other basic functions of the church, and should be given corresponding emphasis in the concern of the church.

4. Christian education is not confined to a church school, but can and should emerge at any point in the church's program, and include everyone in the church's constituency.

5. For the work of Christian education, some are selected to represent the congregation as committee members, officers, and teachers. This important work can never be wholly given over to these representatives, but must be a concern of the whole congregation.

6. The pastor of the church is responsible for a comprehensive ministry, including Christian education. He is the chief Christian educator, assisted in this as in other activities by lay co-workers. The poor condition of Christian education in many churches can be charged to the pastor's failure to accept his whole duty.

7. Christian education consists of those activities whose purpose is the increase of the Christian faith and commitment to discipleship. Its basic content is the Christian gospel, and its method is guided by an understanding of the pupil and how he learns as he confronts the compulsions of the gospel in a multitude of complex human relationships.

8. Christian education results from (1) the experience of being accepted in the fellowship of the Christian congregation and sharing in its worship and work, and (2) participation in the teaching program carried on by the church school.

9. The organization and program of the church school must be such as to provide maximum unity with and dependence on the church as a whole, while at the same time providing an effective educational instrument.

10. Successful work in Christian education is to be measured by the extent to which loyalties to the church and its worship and work have been developed, not by the strength of loyalties to the church school as an institution.

3   ORGANIZING FOR CHRISTIAN EDUCATION

The purpose of organization is to provide a structure through which the church may do its work in Christian education. Organization is secondary to program, but an inadequate or faulty structure may be responsible for ineffectiveness of program.

Organization will be dealt with on two levels: (1) the organization of the church so as to make proper provision for Christian education in its total program; (2) organization within the educational program itself.

It should be made clear at the outset that there is no best type of organization which can be outlined in detail for every situation. Churches differ in denominational polity, size, leadership, and other factors to such an extent that they should find varying ways of applying the principles of good organization to meet their needs. Only those who know the people and the conditions of a particular church can organize wisely for its educational program.

24

ORGANIZING THE CHURCH

The basic problem to be met in church organization is to provide for the most effective carrying on of all its work, while at the same time maintaining unity in its total program and responsibility of the entire congregation for all parts of it. Chart II suggests a plan to accomplish this purpose. With variations it can be applied in any church.

Chart II

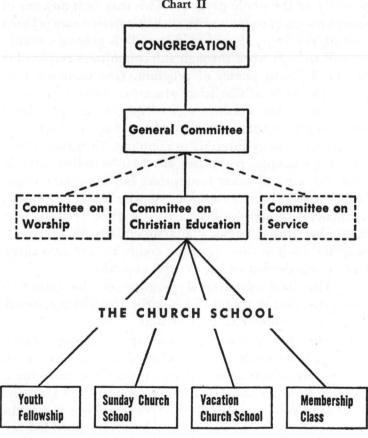

This chart is to be interpreted as follows:

1. The final authority and responsibility for all aspects of the church program, including Christian education, rest with the congregation. The congregation works through boards and committees which it selects by whatever method is prescribed in its constitution or denominational polity.

2. Most churches have a general committee which takes responsibility for the administration, integration, and supervision of the whole program. This may bear any one of several names in common use, such as *official board, church council, consistory, board of elders.* This general committee will in turn work through sub-committees responsible for the different phases of program. One of these is assigned the work of Christian education. Others may deal with evangelism, worship, stewardship, missions, finance and property, community relations, and so on. Such committees have many interests in common. Christian education, for example, permeates all these activities, and in turn, the work of other committees has important implications for Christian education. Hence the need of having the general committee keep them in close relation with each other through review and supervision of the whole program. Each of these program committees should therefore be represented on the general committee.

3. The total educational program of the church is called the *church school.* This is the particular responsibility of the committee on Christian education.

4. The church school is made up of all the agencies whose primary purpose is Christian education. Only a few of these are shown in this chart. A more complete list is given in Charts I and III. Churches vary in the kind and number of such agencies. The important thing is that the work in Christian education be adequately provided for,

that the several agencies be held in such relationship with each other that each may best do what it is capable of doing without too much overlapping with others, and that the entire constituency of the church be related in some way to the work of Christian education.

THE COMMITTEE ON CHRISTIAN EDUCATION

Christian education has its proper place in the total work of the church through a committee which is given responsibility for all the educational work.

1. *Name.* Various names are used to designate this committee, such as Board of Christian Education, Commission on Christian Education, Board of Parish Education, as well as the common name Committee on Christian Education. The name does not matter, as long as its work is understood and its co-ordinate status with other program committees is clearly indicated.

2. *Duties.* In broad terms, it is the work of this committee to plan and maintain a comprehensive program of Christian education in the church. This includes not only the Sunday school but all aspects of the educational program.

Within this broad scope, there will be many specific duties which may be grouped under such headings as: (1) the development of concern for Christian education in the church; (2) adopting educational policies and building a program which is consistent therewith; (3) evaluating and selecting curriculum materials for all educational agencies; (4) providing for the recruiting and training of workers; (5) maintaining cooperative relationships with homes; (6) maintaining relationships with Christian education interests in the denomination and the community; (7) hearing and considering reports from officers and making reports to the church; (8) making and recommending a budget.

3. *Membership.* It must be small enough to function as an informal working group, yet large enough to be fairly representative of the different educational interests. The size may range from five to seven in the smaller church to twelve to fifteen in the larger church. These members should either be elected by the congregation or appointed by the general church committee. The term of office may appropriately be two or three years, with expirations of terms so arranged that not more than one third or one half of the members will be new each year.

In view of its significant work, the members of this committee should be selected with great care, for their interest, experience, and general competence. Some should be active in the church school. Others may be selected because of broad concern with the work of the church as a whole. Some should be parents of pupils in the church school. Some may represent agencies such as adult groups and youth groups, but it should be clear that they are not there as "special pleaders" for the groups they represent, but only to help give a broad basis for understanding the many aspects of the program as a whole. The pastor, director of Christian education, and church school superintendent should be *ex-officio* members.

It is not necessary that all members be trained in Christian education. They need only to be willing to learn. The committee will be continually educating itself in its purpose and work. Through membership in this committee, it may be possible to bring "new blood" into the work of Christian education, and to increase the number of people in the congregation who are concerned with it.

The purpose of the committee on Christian education is

different from that of the meeting of teachers and officers usually called the *workers' conference*. The former is concerned with basic policy and program. The latter is properly a training activity for workers, and when it does have recommendations on policy and program it should clear these through the committee.

The question may be raised whether in a small church it is necessary to have both a committee on Christian education and a workers' conference, since the same people will likely be involved in both. Certainly the committee will be more simply organized and smaller in the small church. It may even be possible for the same group to serve both purposes. However, there is danger that a group consisting of the church school workers only will be so involved with the immediate problems of their work that they are unable to acquire the broad perspective on the whole program which is essential to a committee on Christian education. Even a small church needs to have done the work outlined for a committee on Christian education, as well as the training of workers which can be given in the workers' conference. When these two functions are combined, meetings should be so planned that proper time and attention will be given to both.

4. *Organization and Meetings.* The committee will need a chairman and a recording secretary. The chairman may be designated by the appointing body or elected by the committee. He should represent the committee on the general church committee. Sometimes the pastor, director of Christian education, or church school superintendent is asked to serve as chairman, but it is better to have some other person in this position so as to leave these officers free for participation in meetings.

In a larger church, it is desirable to distribute some of

the work of the committee to sub-committees. One plan is to have sub-committees for certain functions, such as teacher enlistment, curriculum, special days, budget, audio-visuals. Another is to have three age-group sub-committees, dealing respectively with the special interests of children, youth, and adults. There may also be special committees for specific tasks. In all cases, the chairmen of sub-committees should be on the main committee and report to it. Other members may be assigned to sub-committees in accordance with interest and abilities, and non-members may be co-opted to serve on sub-committees as needed.

A committee with such broad scope of work will of necessity meet regularly, and this usually means monthly. The agenda for each meeting should include all items on which immediate action is required, as well as long-range policy discussions. This agenda should be prepared by the chairman in consultation with the pastor, superintendent, and director of Christian education. It is helpful for each member to have a copy of the agenda so that he may participate more intelligently by knowing in advance what is to be covered. The chairman should give "snap" to the meetings by beginning and closing on time, keeping the business moving along according to the agenda, and discouraging aimless talk. The secretary should keep an accurate record of proceedings for future reference.

5. *The Pastor and the Committee.* The pastor is an essential member of the committee on Christian education and should be present at all meetings. As pastor of the church, he can help the committee members keep aware of the place of their work in the total program. His theological training will enable him to help the committee in understanding the meaning of Christian education, and in

matters of the Bible, worship, theology, Christian ethics, and so on. In turn, the committee will help him in achieving his educational ideals for the church.

If the church has a director of Christian education, he will bring similar leadership to the committee as the pastor, but of a more specialized sort. He will be even more intimately related to the committee than is usually possible for the pastor. Yet this should not keep the pastor from attending meetings of the committee and otherwise taking an active interest in its work.

6. *The Superintendent and the Committee.* A committee can deliberate, adopt policies, consider proposals, give guidance, but it cannot engage in the detailed work of administration of the church school. This is the responsibility of the superintendent. Hence he will work under the direction of the committee, and accurately interpret its policies in his administration of the church school.

The superintendent is also an important factor in helping the committee to deal with matters which are of vital concern. He will bring to it important items of policy and program from his field of responsibility on which advice and authorization are needed. He will share in the discussion of such matters. He will keep the committee vitally related to the church school. He may be an elected member of the committee. If this is not the case, he will meet with the committee on an *ex officio* basis.

This does not mean that all details relating to the administration of the church school should be brought before the committee. There are many minor decisions which will be made by the superintendent and his associates, in accordance with policies already established. The superintendent must exercise good judgment in deciding what should have the attention of the committee.

In case the superintendent is responsible for the Sunday school only, and others are at the head of the vacation church school and other agencies, these others will hold the same relationship to the committee when it deals with their respective areas of responsibility.

7. *Starting a New Committee.* Churches that do not yet have a committee on Christian education should remedy this weakness as soon as possible. The pastor and superintendent may work this out together. If the church's constitution or denominational polity provide for such a committee, steps should be taken to carry this provision into effect. Where there is no official provision, appropriate action to establish a committee should be recommended. Sometimes it is good policy to start a committee on an unofficial basis and defer official action for changes in constitution or by-laws until it has demonstrated its usefulness.

A more difficult problem is how to activate a committee which exists on paper but does not meet. This condition usually results from failure to understand its purpose, or short-sightedness of officers in not operating under its guidance. The remedy is for the pastor and superintendent to map out a program of work and then confront the committee with a real job. Committees which sense the significance of their work will usually get busy in doing it.

THE CHURCH SCHOOL

At one time the *Sunday school* was practically the only agency of Christian education. It started outside the church and was only gradually adopted by the church as its own. Since 1914[1] the name *church school* has also been widely used. The new name signified a change in char-

---

[1] The date of publication of Walter S. Athearn's influential book *The Church School.*

acter. More emphasis was now laid on better teaching, better teaching materials, better equipment for teaching. It emphasized the vital relation of Christian education to the church—that it is the church itself engaged in teaching.

During recent years new agencies for Christian education have been developing, such as the young people's society, vacation church school, the weekday church school, summer conferences. At first these new agencies were independent of the church school, but it soon became evident that they are part of the church's educational program. In addition, there are other aspects of the church's work which contribute to Christian education. The name *church school* is now generally applied to this total program. Thus it is emphasized that Christian education is not limited to Sunday morning, but may go on at any time and through many agencies.

Unfortunately, the term *church school* is often also used to mean the Sunday school as well as in its broader sense, thus leading to some confusion. To avoid this confusion, the term *Sunday church school* is now frequently used, but this still does not distinguish it from the youth fellowship which also meets on Sunday. In this book we shall stick to the time-honored name of Sunday school for the Sunday morning program, in spite of some unfortunate implications which it carries.

The Sunday school is the church's most important educational agency in point of numbers enrolled, age-span covered, and its almost universal existence in every church. Most of those who use this book will probably be primarily concerned with the Sunday school. Nevertheless, we cannot be fair in our consideration of Christian education without treating it in its broad application as the total teaching program of the church.

Chart III

DIVISIONS	DEPARTMENTS	Classes: AGE or GRADE
ADULT	Home Dept. / Older Adult / Middle Adult / Young Adult	All ages / 65- / 35-65 / 25-34
YOUTH 12-24	Young People	18-24
	High School (Senior)	XII / XI / X
	Jr. High (Intermediate)	IX / VIII / VII
CHILDREN Birth-11	Junior	VI / V / IV
	Primary	III / II / I
	Kindergarten	4-5
	Nursery Class	2½-3
	Nursery Roll	

AGENCIES:

- SUNDAY SCHOOL
- YOUTH FELLOWSHIP
- VACATION CHURCH SCHOOL
- WEEKDAY CHURCH SCHOOL
- CHURCH MEMBERSHIP CLASSES
- CHOIRS
- THRU-THE-WEEK GROUPS (Cubs / Scouts / Men's & Women's)
- CAMPS, CONFERENCES & CONVENTIONS
- LEADERSHIP, EDUCATION & SERVICE (Officers, Committees, Teachers)
- CHURCH LIBRARY-CHRISTIAN LITERATURE
- THE CHRISTIAN HOME (Home Department / Nursery Roll)

AGE-GROUPS AND AGENCIES

The church school is a complex institution, dealing with all ages and including several agencies. An effective organization of the constituency is required if there is to be order and not chaos. Chart III presents a scheme for the complete organization of the constituency. Suggestions for adaptation in smaller churches will follow. The next few paragraphs should be read in relation to this chart.

1. *Definition of Terms*

(1) *Division* is the term applied to the largest grouping. There are three divisions—one each for children, youth, and adults.

(2) *Department* is the name for the smaller groups within each division. The chart has been drawn to show the customary plan of including three years or grades in each department, except at the pre-school and post-high school levels. Some denominations are now favoring a plan for including only two years or grades in each department, as described in the section "Adaptations in Larger Churches" which follows. Small churches may find it necessary to have even fewer departments and include more than three years in each, while very large churches may need to have departments for each age or school grade.

Each department is a working unit, with a principal and other officers, and usually its own meeting for worship.

The names of the divisions and departments, as well as the ages included in each, have been established through long usage. It is wise to adhere to them as closely as feasible because they are commonly used in discussions of Christian education, and most church school lesson materials are based on them.

(3) *Class* or *grade* is the sub-division within the department for teaching purposes. In smaller churches there may

be just one class to a school grade, or two or more grades may need to be combined to form a class. In larger churches there may be two or more classes in each grade.

The church school class is the smallest unit of organization, providing for intimate relationship between teacher or leader and group. For pupils who are of school age, the day school grade is the best basis for classification rather than the chronological age. It assures that pupils of the same general ability will be working together, and provides for annual promotion to the next higher grade. It avoids the problem of whether a pupil should be advanced on the day of his birthday. Under special circumstances, exceptions may be allowed, as when a pupil is retarded in day school but should remain with his social group in church school. However, too many exceptions will destroy the system of classification.

(4) *Agency* is the name used to designate the several "schools" which together make up the whole church school, such as Sunday school, vacation church school, youth fellowship, young adults. Each of these has its own appeal and makes its own contribution, but needs to be worked into the pattern of the whole. Some of these agencies are completely the responsibility of the committee on Christian education because their primary function is Christian education. Others are not primarily educational in nature, but have educational implications in their program for which they should look to the committee for guidance. The more common agencies are shown in Chart III. Most churches will not have all these, and in some there may be agencies not named here.[2]

---

[2] For a treatment of the educational contributions of these agencies, see *The Church and Christian Education* by Paul H. Vieth, chapter 3. The Bethany Press, 1947.

The portion of the column representing each agency which is not blacked out shows the ages with which it usually works, though there are variations from this. Thus, the Sunday school column has no black portion because it provides for all ages, the vacation school column shows that it usually includes the departments from kindergarten to junior high school, and so with the others.

2. *Adaptations in the Small Church.* Chart III has been drawn to show the complete organization of the church school. Workers in small churches may think that this chart is too elaborate to fit their situation. Let it be granted that adaptations need to be made to fit a particular church. Nevertheless, it is easier to make these adaptations after seeing the total pattern than without it. The traditional age-groupings and department names should be adhered to as closely as possible.

Few church schools will be so small that there cannot be at least one class each for pre-school, primary, junior, junior high, senior high, young people, and adults.

Department organization is usually related to grouping for worship. This in turn is as much affected by rooms available for worship as by numbers. Thus some small schools may of necessity have no division into departments at all, but meet as a whole group. Others may have a department for younger children and a "main school." Whatever combinations of departments necessity dictates will have to be made, but it must not be expected that the same quality of work can be done under these conditions as is possible when pupils of more nearly the same age are working together. Every effort should be made to provide separate department groupings for at least the younger children.

3. *Adaptations in Larger Churches.* Some churches pre-

fer the 2-year plan of department organization in the children's division, and perhaps also throughout the church school. This will make the following pattern: Nursery, age 3 and under; Kindergarten, age 4-5; Primary, grades 1-2; Lower Junior, grades 3-4; Upper Junior, grades 5-6; Junior High, grades 7-8; High School, grades 9-10 and 11-12. This plan has distinct advantages when 2-year departmental graded lessons are used, and works equally well with closely graded. When numbers are very large, it is necessary to have a department for each age or grade, at least through the children's division.

4. *Co-education or Segregation?* The question of co-education or segregation of the sexes arises only at certain ages. There is generally no segregation in departments, in classes for younger children, and in youth fellowships. Segregation is customary in through-the-week clubs because of the nature of the activities. Adult classes often prefer to be segregated, though it is hard to find a good reason for this. The problem narrows down to whether there should be separation of sexes for class work at certain ages.

The arguments for separation run as follows: Social attitudes at certain ages cause boys and men to desire to be grouped with their own kind, and so with girls and women. At certain ages girls are physically and socially more mature than boys. Boys and men should have male teachers and girls and women should have women teachers. Some teachers prefer having only pupils of their own sex.

The arguments against separation include: Church school teaching is about the same for either sex. It is natural for boys and girls to be together because this is the case in the home and the school. Some teachers prefer mixed classes, and pupils may actually respond as well or better to teachers of the opposite sex. Especially in the small church, it is possible to have closer grading with classes of reasonable size when they are mixed.

Granting that there is some weight to the arguments on both sides, it is our conclusion that it is generally better to have mixed groups throughout the church school except for such activities as have a primary appeal to one sex or the other. In the larger church it can make no great difference which plan is followed, but in the smaller church there are distinct advantages in mixed groups for reasons already given.

5. *Size of Groups.* Groups can be too small or too large for most effective work. In pre-school groups, because of the nature of the children and the more informal program, the numbers should not go beyond 12 to 25. In older departments, the worship service can be conducted with numbers anywhere from a few to 50 or even more, though pupil participation is likely to be better if the number is not too large. When departments run beyond 50 to 75, it is wise to consider some division. For good class and club work an intimate relation between pupils with each other and with their leaders is desirable. If groups are too small, the pupils lose interest; if too large, the intimate relationship is lost, and discipline problems are likely to arise.

Policy with respect to size of church school classes varies widely. Some prefer classes of 8 to 10 so as to facilitate personal attention and contact with homes, as well as to reduce problems of discipline. Others feel that classes of 12 to 18 pupils are not only feasible but lead to greater interest and better group response, and by reducing the total number of classes make it easier to have a good teacher and a separate classroom for each class. Some leaders are recommending that primary and junior classes have as many as 25 pupils, with the whole program conducted within the classroom without a department assembly for worship. In this case it is necessary to have a classroom for each class, of sufficient size (20 to 30 square feet per pupil) to allow for varied activity, and two or more teachers for each class. In smaller churches the size of classes will be limited by the number of pupils of a given age, though there are those who consider it possible and even desirable to combine two or three grades in the same teaching group.

6. *Note on Christian Education of Adults.* Some of the foregoing discussion applies more particularly to children's and youth departments than adult. Christian education of adults is a great need. Adults need to continue to learn more about the Bible, the Christian gospel, and the church, so that they may grow up in the faith. They need help in relating religion to the activities, problems, and perplexities of adult life in home, business and profession, politics, community and world relationships. With the rapidly growing numbers of older adults, a new emphasis on church activity especially for them is imperative.

Adult classes in the Sunday school are important elements in the program, but adult Christian education is mediated through many agencies. These include the sermon, men's and women's organizations, lenten series, special lectures and discussions, week-day study groups, parents' meetings, and participation in the boards and committees of the church.

The interests and needs of adults vary at different age levels. Hence the importance of making provision for young adults, young couples, older adults, as well as the great body of the middle aged. Young adults especially find it difficult to make the transition from youth groups to adult if no provision is made for activities for their age-group, and are often lost to the church.

Adults are better able to provide their own leadership than younger groups. What is needed is not so much a leader who can instruct other adults, as a person who can draw others into a process of learning together. Smaller groups in which an intimate relationship can exist and discussion procedures practiced are to be desired above large lecture classes.

Care should be exercised that Sunday school adult groups do not become so large and self-conscious as to rival the church. This is accomplished in one church which has a rule that no adult class may have more than 20 members. As soon as that number is reached, it must divide into two classes, and each exerts itself to build its number up to 20, when the process of division is repeated. Department worship services are not necessary, since adults should have their need for worship met in the congregational service. This makes it possible to have more time for class and group sessions.

CONSTITUTION

A constitution is the official document in which organized bodies set forth their plan of organization and procedure. It provides both the legal limits within which the body must operate and a guide to procedure for those responsible for its work.

The constitution of a church should have an article which defines the place of Christian education in its work and makes organizational provision for carrying it on. It is here that a plan for the committee on Christian education should appear. Three examples follow.

The Methodist Church provides in its *Discipline* for the complete organization of the local congregation. Christian education appears as follows:

#223. In order that a local church may be so organized and administered as to provide effectively for the Christian education of its entire constituency, there shall be a *Commission on Christian Education* in each local church. . . . In a small church the Commission on Christian Education and the Workers' Conference may function as one body except in the election of officers and teachers of the church school.

#226. In each local church there shall be a *church school* for the purpose of discharging the church's responsibility for instructing and guiding its entire constituency in Christian faith and living. The church school shall provide for worship, fellowship, study and service, including social, recreational, evangelistic, and missionary activities, and education in the Holy Scriptures, the Christian religion and the Christian Church.

Other paragraphs in the same section deal in detail with the membership and functions of the commission, the scope and organization of the church school, and the duties of the superintendent. (*Doctrines and Disciplines of the Methodist Church*, 1952, 223-235.)

The Presbyterian Church U.S.A. has by official actions instructed local congregations on making provision for Christian education, from which the following paragraphs are quoted:

The church *Session* is charged with maintaining the spiritual government of the congregation; for which purpose, they have power to inquire into the knowledge and Christian conduct of the members of the church; . . . to concert the best measures for promoting the spiritual interests of the congregation; *to supervise the Sabbath School and the various societies or agencies of the congregation.* (Italics ours.) The responsibility for all the educational work of a particular church is with the pastor and the session, and nothing should be done to lessen their sense of it, but rather, everything should be done to deepen it. Nevertheless, this work is of sufficient importance to justify—indeed, to require—its committal to a committee acting under their authority.

Churches in denominations which have not given such clear direction concerning the place of Christian education in the local church need to devise their own constitutional statements covering this point. The following is an example from a local church constitution:

Article VI: The Christian Education Committee shall consist of its chairman, elected by the church for a term of two years, and at least six members appointed annually by the Church Council, two or more of whom shall represent the church at large and shall not be members of the church school staff. The Pastor, the Minister of Christian Education and the Church School Superintendent (appointed by the Church Council in May of each year) shall be members of this Committee *ex-officiis.*

Under the direction of the Church Council, this Committee shall inaugurate and maintain the religious educational activities of the church. It shall nominate to the Council the Church School Superintendent, the Minister of Christian Education and other employed assistants, and shall appoint and remove teachers and officers of the church school not otherwise provided for. It shall cooperate with other Program Committees in educational activities of common concern.

It is doubtful whether a church school should have a constitution of its own, apart from the general church constitution. Such formal provision may have a tendency to emphasize a separateness from the church which we are trying to avoid. On the other hand, it is desirable to have a written plan of organization and procedure to be followed in maintaining the church school. Most denominations provide printed materials to guide local workers in this.[3]

---

[3] The following are good examples:

Christian Education in Our Church, Presbyterian USA

Organizing for Christian Education in the Church, Evangelical and Reformed. This offers suggested by-laws for a church constitution, to include Christian education.

Organization and Program of the Methodist Church School

Parish Education, United Lutheran Church

4 DUTIES OF COMMITTEE, OFFICERS, AND TEACHERS

The active church school has many workers. Each has his own duties and all are in relation to each other in a common purpose. Good organization and administration must do more than devise a smoothly operating machine. It must also develop a fellowship of workers in which each feels a warm relationship to all the others and senses the importance of his work.

The most effective administrative officer is not the one who can only give executive direction from the top down. There should be two-way communication. General officers will regard others on the staff as co-workers who are partners in a common task, and will accept suggestions from them as well as giving them general direction. Church school workers are first of all Christian persons and should be accepted as fellows in the proper spirit of a Christian community.

The purpose of this chapter is to list in some detail the

45

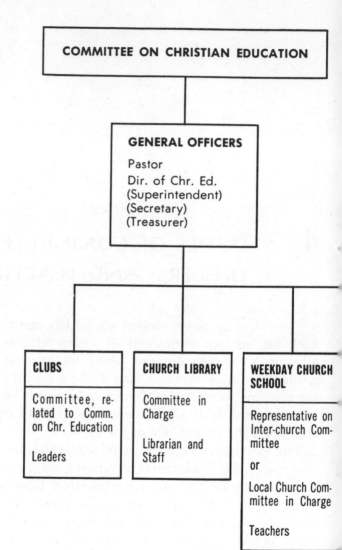

COMMITTEE ON CHRISTIAN EDUCATION

GENERAL OFFICERS

Pastor
Dir. of Chr. Ed.
(Superintendent)
(Secretary)
(Treasurer)

CLUBS

Committee, related to Comm. on Chr. Education

Leaders

CHURCH LIBRARY

Committee in Charge

Librarian and Staff

WEEKDAY CHURCH SCHOOL

Representative on Inter-church Committee

or

Local Church Committee in Charge

Teachers

Chart IV

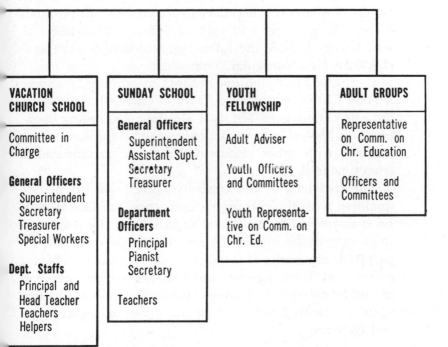

VACATION CHURCH SCHOOL

Committee in Charge

General Officers
Superintendent
Secretary
Treasurer
Special Workers

Dept. Staffs
Principal and Head Teacher
Teachers
Helpers

SUNDAY SCHOOL

General Officers
Superintendent
Assistant Supt.
Secretary
Treasurer

Department Officers
Principal
Pianist
Secretary

Teachers

YOUTH FELLOWSHIP

Adult Adviser

Youth Officers and Committees

Youth Representative on Comm. on Chr. Ed.

ADULT GROUPS

Representative on Comm. on Chr. Education

Officers and Committees

duties of the committee on Christian education and of the officers and other workers, and to show the relationship between them. The remaining chapters will be devoted to an elaboration of what is involved in carrying out these duties. Chart IV shows how the committee on Christian education and the officers and other workers are interrelated in the total church school.

DUTIES OF THE COMMITTEE ON CHRISTIAN EDUCATION

In the previous chapter the purpose and organization of the committee on Christian education have been presented. It is responsible for providing and maintaining the most extensive and effective program of Christian teaching (church school) of which the church is capable. Its duties consist of whatever is necessary to accomplish this purpose. Its specific activities will vary in different churches, but will usually include the following, which may serve as a check list for a particular committee:

1. *Study.* The committee needs to inform itself on what is good Christian education. This is especially important for a new committee, but must also be a continuing interest. This book may serve as a basic manual for such study, together with other resources which are recommended from time to time.

The members of the committee need also to be acquainted with the existing church school, so that it may be evaluated in light of good practice and the needs for improvement discovered. This acquaintance will come in part from experience of members in the work of the church school and from reports made to the committee, but should be enlarged by having committee members observe what is actually being done in the different departments and agencies.

2. *Policy Making.* Policy consists of general operating principles under which effective practice may be developed. Basic to all policy is a statement of objectives of the church school. Policy decisions are also involved in dealing with such problems as: How integrate the contributions of the several agencies into the broad conception of the church school? What new agencies are needed? What type of curriculum shall be used? What standards shall be established for the church school and for workers? How shall the church school be related to the general service of worship? What financial plan shall be adopted? How shall the church school be related to the homes? What department and class organization is best? What requirements for enrollment and standards of attendance shall be established?

3. *Organization.* This has two aspects: (1) the improvement of existing organization, such as better department and class grouping, closer relation of agencies to the total program, and (2) providing for agencies which do not yet exist, such as a vacation church school, participation in camps and conferences, a day nursery school, young adult groups, parent-teacher activities, co-operation in community activities such as leadership schools and weekday church schools.

4. *Workers.* The responsibility for enlisting, appointing, training, and guiding workers for all phases of the educational program (except officers elected by youth and adult groups themselves) falls to this committee. The actual performance of this function may in part be carried out by sub-committees and general officers. A sub-committee on workers may make a continuous study of leadership needs and available persons, and after approval by the committee, enlist the workers and provide training opportunities for them.

5. *Curriculum.* The committee should choose the curriculum materials. Usually this will mean adopting the material provided by its own denomination but even so, a choice must be made because most denominations publish more than one system of lessons. Selection must be followed by training of the workers in understanding the material and making proper use of it. Moreover, the published curriculum should be supplemented by other resources, such as activity materials, missions material, background books for teachers, audio-visual aids, supplies such as pencils and paper. The plan for providing such materials is the responsibility of the committee, but the details of making them available to workers will be left to the administrative officers. Under curriculum may also be included the observance of special days, and proper emphasis on evangelism, missions, social problems, Christian family life, and church membership. In these latter areas of interest there are usually other committees with which the committee on Christian education needs to cooperate. For example, the Christian service committee may wish to promote such a program as *One Great Hour of Sharing.* Since this has Christian education values and affects the church school, the two committees need to work out the plans together.

6. *Space and Equipment.* Inadequacy of space and equipment is a handicap to Christian education in most churches. Attention to this problem will involve the committee in such considerations and decisions as (1) the best placement of groups so as to make maximum use of what is available; (2) re-arrangement of time schedules so that the same rooms may be used more than once on Sunday morning; (3) purchase of new equipment when needed; (4) a long-range program for improvement, in some cases involving re-modeling and new construction.

7. *Enlistment.* The church school is the best recruiting agency for the church. While a first duty is to provide properly for those who are already members and encourage their regular attendance, the committee must be alert to enlisting others who have not been reached with Christian teaching. Systematic plans for enlistment should supersede the pious hope that "if they are interested they will come" or the complacent conclusion "we already have more than we can handle."

8. *Records.* Adequate records, carefully kept and regularly reported, are basic to improving the program. While the keeping of the records is the work of the church school secretary, the committee must see to it that a good system of records is used, that a competent secretary is in charge, and that the facts which the records reveal are used by itself and the workers in the church school.

9. *Budget.* If the church has accepted the church school as its own, it will normally provide for it in the annual budget. The committee on Christian education is responsible for making an estimate of needs and recommending a proposed budget to the finance committee. When the budget for Christian education is approved, the committee must supervise its administration. If the church has not yet accepted Christian education in its budget, steps should be taken to effect this as soon as possible.

From this analysis of duties, it is clear that this committee is the body in which power is vested to transact the necessary business of the church school. Some matters may be referred to the workers for discussion and recommendation, but the committee is responsible for the final decisions. Workers groups and individuals may also initiate recommendations for consideration of the committee. Pupils will have no part in the election of officers and teachers and the transaction of general church school business. Their opportunity to share in the democratic process comes in relation to the internal life and activities of their classes, departments, and fellowship groups.

DUTIES OF GENERAL OFFICERS

By general officers we mean those who, under the direction of the committee on Christian education, have responsibility for the administration and supervision of the entire church school, or the whole program of an agency within the church school. There is a total job of administration that must be done, in which all the general officers share as a team, each contributing as he is able and in accordance with the assignment of duties made to him. Following is a list of the general offices which exist in most church schools, together with the duties usually performed by those filling these offices.

1. *Pastor.* The pastor is much more than a general officer of the church school, but in relation to Christian education he functions in this capacity. It is an unfortunate situation for the church as well as for the church school when Christian education is left almost wholly to lay workers. The work of the pastor will vary with the situation which exists in different churches. Where lay leadership is at a low ebb he needs to give more of his time to the church school than is necessary where strong lay leadership is available. In any situation, however, the following contributions should be made by him.

(1) *Educate the whole church in the nature and importance of Christian education, through*

    (a) Preaching on Christian education and using good educational method in working with boards, committees and other groups.

(b) Stressing the importance of the church school as a vital part of all that the church is and does.

(c) Helping parents to see their responsibility for Christian education in the home and their necessary part in making the church school effective.

(d) Impressing on each church member that the church's teaching work deserves and needs his support.

(e) Developing and maintaining a church organization which properly provides for Christian education.

(2) *Inspire and support the work of the committee on Christian education, through*

(a) Attending its meetings.

(b) Giving the spiritual and educational leadership for which his professional training has qualified him.

(c) Helping with the development of curriculum and the selection of lesson materials and resources.

(d) Encouraging the inclusion of missions, stewardship, and other program emphases as part of the curriculum.

(3) *Cooperate in the enlistment and training of a staff of workers, through*

(a) Helping the committee on personnel to find prospective workers among the members of the congregation.

(b) Counseling with teachers on problems of Bible and religious interpretation, as well as on effective method.

(c) Training department leaders in the meaning and method of worship, so that worship and worship training in the church school may be improved; providing for inter-relation between church school and church worship; arranging family services.

(d) Teaching training classes, especially in subjects for which his own professional training best fits him.

(e) Encouraging the holding of effective workers' conferences and participating in the program.

(f) Counseling with the superintendent and other officers on matters of administration, supervision, and training.

(4) *Share in the continuing work of the church school, through*

(a) Visiting classes and departments, and at times sharing in their work, though not on regular assignment as a teacher on Sunday morning.

(b) Teaching the church membership class, youth and adult groups which meet at other times than Sunday morning.

(c) Taking an active interest in the work of the youth fellowship.

(d) Sharing in the work of the vacation church school, and perhaps teaching in the weekday church school.

(e) Accepting the need for giving more time to a church school while it is "getting on its feet," but relinquishing this leadership to lay workers as they become trained for it.

(5) *Develop desirable home-church relations in Christian education, through*

(a) Interpreting the work of the church school on his parish calls.

(b) Helping teachers to make contacts with homes, and informing them of home situations which will lead to better understanding of pupils.

(c) Counseling with parents on problems of Christian education.

(d) Encouraging the holding of parent-teacher conferences.

The question may properly be asked, How can a minister do all this in addition to all his other duties? Four answers may be given to this question: (1) Christian education is so essentially a part of all that the church is and does that no minister can conscientiously give a minor place to leadership in the church school ; (2) in this as in all aspects of church work, except those which require an ordained minister, he will inspire and train lay workers to carry as much of the load as possible; (3) the church school staff represents an opportunity to train a considerable number of lay men and women in a better understanding of religion and to inspire participation in Christian work, which is at the very heart of a pastor's work with people; (4) every church that is able to do so should have a director of Christian education to assist the minister in giving adequate leadership to Christian education.

2. *Director of Christian Education.* A director of Christian education, also called minister of Christian education if he is ordained, either man or woman, is employed by the church to give his whole attention to Christian education. Since only a small percent of churches are financially able to employ a director in addition to the minister, we shall not here state his duties in detail. It is important, however, that churches employing a director first make a clear statement concerning his position and work.[1] Many failures have resulted because this was not done.

In general, the director will give more intensive attention to many of the duties listed above for the pastor, and

---

[1] For guidance in this, see the booklet *The Pastor, The Director of Christian Education and the Sunday School Superintendent: A Team.* National Council of Churches, New York. 10 cents.

those which follow for the superintendent. The pastor should not assume that he is relieved of all educational responsibility, but should continue to work in close relationship with the director and the committee on Christian education.

3. *Church School Superintendent.* Ideally this officer should be the superintendent of the entire church school. In one denomination his responsibility is so defined. However, for most laymen or laywomen it is difficult to take such broad administrative and supervisory responsibility. It is more common to have a superintendent for the Sunday school and corresponding officers for the other agencies. This alternative is shown in Chart IV by placing the word "superintendent" in parenthesis where it appears in relation to the whole church school, and repeating it under Sunday school.

What follows in this chapter will be slanted primarily to the Sunday school, with a few references to broader application. The same analysis of duties will apply to those heading other agencies but in lesser measure, because no other agency has such a large constituency or so complex an organization as the Sunday school.

The superintendent is the general executive and administrative officer; he is responsible for having an effectively organized and smoothly running school. Whatever must be done to achieve this is his work, either directly or through his co-workers. Much of his work will be done through the week. His qualifications should be primarily those of an executive, and whether he combines with this the qualities of orator and platform leader is a secondary matter, as will be evident from the following analysis of his duties. If he is a prominent person in the church, this will help give prestige to the church school, but more important than this is that he be a competent, consecrated, and dedicated person. Whether the superintendent be a man or a woman makes no difference, as long as the best person for the job is appointed. Bearing in mind that his responsibility is for a total job which cannot wholly be included in a list of specific duties, and that his effectiveness is measured by the extent to which he is able to enlist the cooperation of his co-workers, the superintendent's duties may be analyzed to include at least the following:

(1) Serve as executive officer to the committee on Christian education by bringing to it matters which require its consideration, and carrying out its decisions.

(2) Organize an effective Sunday school and maintain the organization. This includes its division into departments and classes, the enrollment and assignment of new pupils, and a plan for annual promotions.

(3) Nominate department principals, teachers, and other workers to the committee on Christian education.

(4) Give inspiration and guidance to teachers and other workers, especially to those who have been newly appointed.

(5) Provide curriculum materials and other resources for all workers, and when necessary, instruct them in their use.

(6) Plan for and usually preside at general workers' conferences.

(7) Provide training opportunities, and encourage workers to attend training schools and conferences.

(8) On authorization of the committee on Christian education, provide new equipment; see that all equipment is kept in good repair, in cooperation with the caretaker; make sure that the building is in order and ready for all sessions.

(9) Supervise the keeping of records and utilize the records for improvement of the school.

(10) Make reports to the committee on Christian education, the workers' conference, the congregation, and parents.

(11) Establish friendly relationships with the homes represented in the church school; help arrange for parents' meetings.

(12) Visit departments and classes; keep informed on what is going on throughout the school; assist other workers when this is desirable, but always with their cooperation, not over their heads.

(13) Make sure that every group has a teacher or leader for all sessions, by assisting in the enlistment of workers and providing substitutes when necessary.

(14) Plan for increasing enrollment by enlisting as many as possible of the church constituency as well as others in the community who do not belong to other churches; supervise follow-up of absent pupils.

(15) Establish friendly contacts with new pupils and their parents, and as far as possible, be acquainted with and show friendly interest in all pupils.

(16) Arrive early for Sunday school sessions and be available as needed to guide smooth operation throughout the session; on occasion, assist with worship and class teaching so as to keep in close contact with the on-going work, but never on regular assignment.

(17) In small schools, where there is a combined worship service, or a "main school" worship service, serve as leader of this service or make provision for others to do so.

(18) In some cases, represent the church school on the general church committee or official board.

(19) Work in close cooperation with the minister and the director of Christian education.

(20) Keep up with new trends and ideas by reading books and magazines on Christian education, and attending conferences.

How long should the superintendent hold office? Like all other workers, he is subject to annual appointment. During his first year he will have many things to learn, so that he will usually be more effective in his second and subsequent years. A superintendent who does the job well, keeps his interest and remains alive to new ideas should normally serve for a period of years. If in his first year he does not give evidence of creative leadership, even a one-year term is too long.

Most churches find it desirable to have an *assistant superintendent* to take the place of the superintendent in his absence and to help him with his numerous duties. Specific duties may be assigned to the assistant. One denomination makes him responsible for membership cultivation. Depending on his particular abilities, he may be put in charge of curriculum, workers' training, guidance of individual workers, or some other of the major duties of the superintendent listed above. Such specific assignment of duties will enhance the importance of the office of assistant superintendent.

4. *Church School Secretary.* It is desirable to have a secretary for the whole church school. Many persons hold membership in more than one agency, and the record should show their complete relationship to the educational program. Also, a unified system of records helps to keep the several agencies and their programs in proper relationship. When there is such a unified plan, the secretaries of each of the agencies will act as assistants to the general sec-

retary, reporting to him for their respective agencies. In many cases there will be a separate system of records for each agency, and a secretary responsible only to it.

The duties of the secretary may be simply stated as (1) establishing a system of records which is adequate, (2) keeping an accurate record, (3) making the facts revealed by the records readily available to all who should be guided by them. This simple statement of duties of the secretary is not a measure of the importance of his work, for he is one of the most important officers in the church school. Church school records will be more fully treated in chapter 14.

5. *Church School Treasurer.* If Christian education is included in the general church budget, it is desirable that the offerings made in the church school be handled by the church treasurer like any other income. Some churches provide a single weekly offering envelope which may be given at any one of the services where an offering is collected. Under this plan the treasurer of the Sunday school or of any other agency serves as assistant to the church treasurer, for the handling of the offerings from that particular agency. If there is a separate budget for the Sunday school or other agency, its treasurer is responsible for handling the funds.

Since the church school offering is more important as a means of teaching Christian stewardship than for the money it yields, explanation of the grounds for Christian giving and the causes which are supported is an important part of curriculum. The treasurer may take the lead in devising ways in which this may best be done in departments and classes.

6. *Cabinet.* Because of the need for frequent consultation on the matters of general administration, some

churches provide for a church school cabinet, consisting of the general officers and the department principals. The time required for meetings is justified by the mutual support and better co-ordination which will result.

DEPARTMENT OFFICERS

Some denominations recommend that the church school have *division superintendents* for children, youth, and adults. Each of these will act as an assistant to the general superintendent for all the work pertaining to his particular division. He will usually represent his division on the committee on Christian education. He may organize a council of all the workers in his division so as to function as a committee for that division. That is a good way to assure co-ordination of the program of all the agencies working with a particular division. In a smaller church this may be all the organization that is necessary, while in larger churches there will be departments within these divisions.

The more usual plan is to organize by departments, or combinations of departments, as suggested in Chart III. The head of each department, whom we shall call *principal* to distinguish him from the general superintendent (though the term *superintendent* is also in general use) may be assisted by a secretary, pianist, and in some cases other officers.

1. *Department Principals.* The department principal is in two-fold relationship, to the committee on Christian education and general officers, and to the workers and pupils in his department. In the former capacity he shares in making and carrying into effect the policies and program for the whole church school. In the latter, he administers and supervises his own department so as to make

it an effective unit in the program of Christian education. The duties of department principals in many cases duplicate those given for general officers, because within the department the principal represents the general officer in carrying them out. These duties may be analyzed as follows:

(1) Cooperate with the general officers in all matters of administration as they apply to his department.

(2) Be thoroughly familiar with the curriculum materials, and administer the curriculum within the department; provide for education in missions and stewardship.

(3) Cooperate in the enlistment and training of workers for the department.

(4) Hold department planning sessions, and counsel with individual workers.

(5) Encourage workers to attend conferences, training classes, conventions and summer schools; provide them with books and magazines which will help in improving their work.

(6) See that curriculum materials and needed supplies, including audio-visual aids, are readily available to all workers.

(7) Check on rooms and equipment before each session to see that everything is in order.

(8) Maintain time schedules which provide for the maximum use of the time available.

(9) Conduct worship services for the department or arrange for others to do this; provide for education in the meaning of worship.

(10) Provide for pupil participation in the department by having committees of pupils; in youth and adult departments, counsel with officers and committees which

have been elected by the established processes in those departments.

(11) Maintain relationship with the homes, including plans for parent-teacher meetings.

(12) Provide substitutes for absent teachers, and be prepared to act as a substitute in case of emergency.

(13) Cooperate with general officers in keeping accurate records, encouraging regular attendance, and following up absent pupils.

(14) Provide for social and recreational activities.

(15) Maintain a friendly atmosphere, orderly procedures, and good discipline.

Our attempt to make one list of duties of department principals is not entirely satisfactory, because these will vary somewhat with the age of the pupils. Youth and adult departments make much larger provision for student participation through election of their own officers and committees than is the case with children. Hence the principal's function as adviser and coordinator becomes more important. Also, older pupils are more likely to be members of other agencies in addition to the Sunday school, thus pointing up the need for seeing the work of these departments in the perspective of the whole church school.

2. *Department Secretaries.* Larger church schools will find it helpful to have a secretary for each department. These will serve as assistants to the general secretary. They will distribute and collect class record books, enroll new pupils, call attention of teachers to prolonged absences of pupils, and in some cases prepare the statistical summary for the department. They may help with the distribution of materials to teachers and relay the department offering to the treasurer.

DUTIES OF TEACHERS

Teachers are in the most intimate relation to pupils. The success of the church school depends largely on them. Everything possible should be done administratively to free them for their work of teaching. Teachers may be expected to do at least the following:

1. Attend regularly, be present well in advance of the opening of each session, and notify the department principal as soon as possible of any anticipated absence.

2. Faithfully teach the established curriculum, with only such modifications as their particular abilities and the needs of the class make desirable.

3. Participate in the service of worship, and encourage pupils in proper participation and good behavior.

4. Take a personal interest in each pupil and his development; follow up on absent pupils.

5. Keep in close touch with homes, including at least one personal visit each year.

6. Keep an accurate record of attendance and other items requested by the secretary.

7. Attend workers' conferences, department staff meetings, training classes, and cooperate in efforts to improve the church school.

OTHER AGENCIES

What has preceded has been slanted strongly to the Sunday school. A few additional notes are in order on other agencies.

1. *Vacation Church School.* Since this is not a continuous activity but a once-a-year program, the committee on Christian education may appoint a sub-committee early in the year to plan and conduct it. The school will be in

immediate charge of a superintendent, who will have other officers and department principals and their assistants to work with him. Their relationships and duties will be much the same as in the Sunday school. If several churches cooperate in holding a vacation church school, the committee on Christian education should be represented on a joint committee which has charge of the co-operative enterprise.

2. *Weekday Church School.* This is usually conducted on an interdenominational basis. The local church should cooperate through a representative on the inter-church body which is responsible for conducting it. If it is a local church school, procedure may be much the same as in the case of the vacation church school.

3. *Youth Fellowship.* An adult adviser for each youth group should be appointed by the committee on Christian education, and a youth representative should be a member of this committee. The youth fellowship should not exist in isolation, but be a part of the youth division of the church school, with a youth superintendent and a council of all youth workers.

4. *Adult Groups.* There may be a superintendent of adult work, corresponding to the youth adviser, but most adult groups outside the Sunday school are able to provide their own leadership. To assure integration with the whole church school, adults should be represented on the committee on Christian education. As with youth work, there should be a council representing all adult groups, and the representative may be chosen from this council.

5. *Nursery Roll and Home Department.* These are agencies to maintain relationship with those too young to attend church school sessions, or prevented from attending for other reasons. The committee on Christian educa-

tion should appoint the superintendents for these departments and support them in their work.

6. *Church Library.* This is related to the educational program, because the chief purposes of having a library are (1) to provide reading material through which the people of the church may become better informed on matters of religion and related subjects, and (2) to provide books and magazines to help the workers in the church school. The committee on Christian education should therefore be responsible for the library and appoint a librarian and assistants.

7. *Scouts and Other Groups.* Such club activities may have important implications for Christian education, and when they are conducted under the auspices of the church should have some relation to the committee on Christian education. Maintaining such relationship is complicated by such factors as: (1) their membership is usually on a community basis irrespective of local church connection, (2) their national headquarters may require that there be an independent committee for such agencies, and (3) men and women who are most interested and competent in such activities sometimes have no close relation to the church school. Relationship may be established by having the committees responsible for such agencies have representation on the committee on Christian education and report to it.

8. *Choirs.* The ministry of music makes an important contribution to Christian education, both to participants and to the worshiping congregation. Hence choirs, especially of children and youth, should be so related to the church school that their work can be a part of the curriculum. Sometimes this can be accomplished by having the choirs sponsored as a part of the church school. More

often they are under the church committee on music and choir director, and at worst may be an exploitation of children for the enjoyment of adults. Sometimes they actually interfere with the church school by demanding rehearsals or performance when the church school is in session. On the other hand, the minister of music may understand Christian education and make a real contribution to it.

MANUAL OF PROCEDURE

How shall the workers in Christian education be made aware of their duties and relationships? One way of doing this is to prepare a simple manual of procedure which will be given to each new worker when he is appointed. Such a manual can be based on what has been presented in this chapter, simplified and adapted to cover the situation in the church where it is to be used. The preparation of such a manual could be an interesting and useful experience for the committee on Christian education, in the course of which many policy decisions would need to be made.

One example of a manual of procedure which has come to our notice covers the following items (details omitted):

Purpose: To make the work of officers and teachers easier through having a definite way of doing things

Item 1 : Hours of church school sessions

Item 2 : Pupils: ages, enrollment procedure, attendance standards, discipline

Item 3 : Use of facilities

Item 4 : Organization of the church school, terms of office, etc.

Item 5 : Duties of officers and teachers

Item 6 : Supplies

5 THE CURRICULUM OF CHRISTIAN EDUCATION

The important thing in Christian education is what happens to people. Organization and administration are necessary, but their value is to be judged by the extent to which they provide a setting in which learners may grow in Christian discipleship.

The basic nature of Christian education is the same in all kinds of churches, but there are vast differences among churches in the extent and complexity of the program which they maintain. A small church may have a simple program compared to that in some larger church. Each must work in accordance with its resources. This does not mean that the program in a small church is necessarily less effective. Some of the elements which make a program most effective, such as Christian fellowship and intimate personal contacts, may be more prominent in a small church just because it is small. Every church, before God, is responsible to do the best it can with the resources it has.

THE NATURE OF CURRICULUM

The word *curriculum* is commonly used for the program of Christian education. Taken in this broad sense, the curriculum is the answer to such questions as: How can we help our pupils to be confronted by and respond to the Christian gospel? How will they best come into saving relationship with Jesus Christ? How can they be helped to grow into the life and work of the church, and to bear Christian witness to the world? Whatever is done for, with, and by the members of the church school to achieve these ends is the curriculum.

By this definition, curriculum is something more than printed lesson materials. It is a living experience of persons in Christian fellowship as they confront God and seek to know and do his will, under the guidance of Christian teachers.

If we knew just what experiences are most influential for growth in Christian discipleship, the problems of curriculum making would be comparatively easy. The process is very complex, and there are factors in it which are not under human control. Christian faith is a gift of God. He works in mysterious ways, and may perform his wonders of redemption through unexpected means and in unlikely places. We cannot compel him to do our will, but must seek to know and to do his will. Yet we know that in his wisdom God does use the witness and work of Christians—parents, ministers, teachers—as channels of grace, through his Holy Spirit. It is clear that such influences as the following contribute to growth in discipleship, and should be utilized in the curriculum.

1. *Christian Fellowship.* The experience of being part of a Christian group is one of the ways by which the

Christian faith is communicated. What was said in chapter 2 about the importance of the Christian community in Christian education should be recalled here.

Christian fellowship is not a part of the curriculum in the sense that it is a subject to be taught. It is a spirit and atmosphere which should pervade the whole program. Its significance in curriculum is two-fold: (1) making provision for pupils in the church school to share as fully as possible in the fellowship of the congregation, (2) fostering this same fellowship in every department, class and group, so that each may be a little *koinonia* (community of love), representing the spirit of the whole church. Actually, the smaller group with its more intimate relationships is more effective in developing the fellowship than whole-church gatherings. This applies in particular to work with younger children, for whom the church school class or department may be the most real expression of the Christian fellowship. Thus in the kindergarten, the relationship which prevails among members, and between leaders and pupils, does more to communicate the Christian faith than any formal teaching.

2. *Christian Persons.* Christian faith is communicated by persons to other persons. The effectiveness of the curriculum depends to a large extent on the contacts it provides for pupils with persons who are dynamic and consecrated Christians. This impact of Christian personality may come through parents, teachers and officers, other persons in the congregation, visitors who share in the program from time to time, and through biographies of great Christian personalities.

3. *Subject Matter.* While objectives are centered in helping pupils to live as disciples, there is a vast amount of subject matter that must be taught as a means to this

end. The Bible is the pre-eminent subject matter for Christian education, and there are some who feel that nothing else is important; but there are other fields of knowledge which must be included, such as the church and its history, Christian beliefs, the arts, the application of the Christian faith to personal and social problems.

4. *Worship*. Christian education is education for life with God. The worship of God is a proper expression for any Christian group which includes God as a participant in its fellowship. This is true for pupils of all ages.

Worship is included in the curriculum because it is a normal part of the life of a Christian group, but also because the meaning and practice of worship need to be learned. Learning to worship comes best through participation in worship, but this participation is enhanced by teaching about worship which helps the pupil to understand its meaning, the proper attitude of the worshiper, and to become familiar with the hymns, responses, prayers, and other elements which make up an order of service.

The curriculum should provide for worship in church school classes and departments, and also for some participation in the general church service of worship. A later chapter will be concerned with ways and means of making worship an effective part of the curriculum.

5. *Christian Work*. Faith in God through Christ, worship, and Christian service are the marks of discipleship. The curriculum must teach the meaning of Christian living and give practice in Christian work.

The most important witness which the Christian gives to his faith is through his whole life—work, play, family life, community activities, and all the many relationships of being a person in a human society. Christian education that is effective always has a meaningful relation to the pupil's whole life, both in his present setting and in preparation for the long future.

Christian living includes participation in service activities which are the concern of the church and its people. Hence the curriculum will teach church work, missions, social service and action, and stewardship. Such teaching will be done both through study of the meaning and importance of such activities and through opportunities for actual participation.

6. *Evangelism.* The beginning of discipleship is commitment to God through Christ, and dedication to doing his will and work. There has been much controversy as to whether such commitment comes through a single conversion experience or whether it may result from Christian nurture which seeks orientation toward God from childhood. Without entering this controversy, let us assert that (1) a true disciple has no doubt about having committed his whole being to God and having been accepted by God, and (2) he needs to have many re-commitments as he grows in fuller understanding of God's will and fuller participation in the complex life of the world with all its temptation.

Evangelism is not limited to occasional opportunities for decision and commitment. It is an aim which is present throughout the curriculum of Christian education. Evangelism may be more prominent at certain times and places, such as the Easter season, in the confirmation class, in preparation for baptism of young people and adults, but it may come to fruition at many other points, through Bible study, worship, fellowship, and service activities.

7. *Method.* Educational method is in a sense only the way in which workers deal with pupils and subject matter. Method nevertheless has a profound influence on what

happens to persons, and should never be described as "mere" method. The importance of method will be clear from the implications of such questions as: Does the leader do everything for the pupils, or allow them to participate? Is his chief concern with the material which he wants the pupil to learn or is he first concerned with what the pupil most needs? Is discipline maintained by harsh control or is it the result of a loving, cooperative spirit between workers and pupils? Does the group provide for genuine fellowship through which each member may develop as a person or is it dominated by rivalries, argument, irrelevant conversation, or general disinterest? Are opportunities provided for sharing in Christian work or is there only pious talk about such matters? Is respectable work required or do the pupils "get away with anything"? Does the teaching of the Bible make it only a record of the exploits of ancient people or a living Word for today?

These are some of the important factors which influence growth in Christian discipleship. When they are worked out as a planned program they constitute the curriculum of Christian education. Thus the curriculum is a living experience which results when workers and learners together seek to understand and practice the Christian life.

We have made a distinction between curriculum as living experience and published curriculum materials. Published materials have an important place in curriculum, but they are only the basis for the curriculum, not the curriculum itself. They are tools for the use of the local church in making its curriculum.

PUBLISHED CURRICULUM MATERIALS

Curriculum materials are prepared and published by denominational boards of Christian education, and some other publishers, to provide the basis for the program of Christian education in the church. Through this means competent individuals and committees are able to do for churches what most of them are not able to do for themselves.

1. *Purpose.* Published materials help local churches in such important ways as the following:

(1) They provide an organized program, based on the purpose and nature of Christian education, including all that is most important for this purpose.

(2) They make readily available the subject matter needed, such as selections from and interpretation of the Bible, worship, evangelism, missions, the church, personal and social problems, and service projects, all in proper relation to each other and in desirable balance.

(3) They arrange the content of the curriculum in graded order of increasing difficulty to allow for the pupils' advancing age and growing knowledge.

(4) They provide local church workers with an interpretation of religious problems which is in harmony with the theological outlook and witness of their denomination.

(5) They are published in suitable books, booklets or magazines, so as to make the necessary content readily available to workers and pupils.

(6) For general and departmental officers, they provide worship materials and other suggestions to help in the administration of the curriculum for the whole church school, and the several departments.

(7) For teachers, they provide manuals which give the necessary help in teaching a course, usually on a quarterly basis. These include the scope of the whole course, divided into suitable units and weekly sessions. For each

session they give the objective, content, suggestions for suitable methods, and additional resources, such as pictures and worksheets.

(8) For pupils they provide the content which they need, suggestions for study, and material for activities, such as workbooks.

(9) So far as possible, everything needed by teachers and pupils is included in the published material, but references are made to other sources which may be found in the church library, the public library, or in other available places.

2. *Types.* Published curriculum or program materials are available for Sunday schools, vacation church schools, weekday church schools and youth fellowships. Materials for Sunday schools are organized by one of three plans:

(1) *Closely Graded Lessons* follow the public school plan of grading by single years, so as to fit the ability and experience of each pupil most closely. Some publishers make suggestions for using their closely graded materials on a group graded basis in smaller churches.

Weekday church school materials are usually closely graded, but some are on a two-year graded system so that the pupils from two grades may be combined in one class if necessary, and the two courses taught in alternate years.

(2) *Group Graded Lessons* (also called "departmental graded" and "cycle graded") are uniform within each department, but have different material for the different departments. On any given Sunday the pupils in one department, such as the primary, have the same lesson, while the pupils in other departments have different lessons. Thus it is possible for such lessons to be graded to meet the abilities and needs of pupils in each department.

Group grading is by either two-year or three-year cycles.

To use such materials most successfully, the Sunday school should be organized by two-year or three-year departments, to correspond to the organization of the lesson materials. Since at the end of any given cycle all the pupils in a given department will have advanced to the next higher department, there is no repetition of the same materials as far as the pupils are concerned. Some publishers have established a theme, such as the Bible, the Life of Christ, the Church, for a given year throughout the church school so as to provide unity for the curriculum as a whole. Adaptations of the theme are made for each department to suit the age and ability of the pupils.

For the special benefit of small church schools, one denomination publishes *broadly graded* materials which provide for only four age groups.

Vacation church school materials, and those for youth groups, are usually group graded.

(3) *Uniform Lessons* provide a common core of Bible material for all ages throughout the Sunday school. Adaptations are made for each department, with supplementary material suited to the age of the pupils.

(4) *Elective Materials.* In addition to the above *series,* some publishers provide elective units for young people and adults, which may be substituted under certain conditions for series materials.

Since this book has been written for use by all denominations, it is not practical to illustrate the above types of curriculum materials by actual reference to the types published by a particular denomination. The following summary may help to overcome this deficiency: Almost all denominations publish uniform lessons; group graded lessons are published by the United Church of Christ (Congregational Christian and Evangelical and Reformed),

Evangelical United Brethren, Methodist, Presbyterian, United Church of Canada, United Lutheran; closely graded lessons are published by American Baptist, Disciples of Christ, Methodist, Protestant Episcopal, Southern Baptist.

3. *Comparative Merits of Each Type.* There are arguments which may be advanced in favor of each of these plans of organization and grading of curriculum materials.

Closely graded lessons follow the best educational procedure in relating the curriculum to each year in the pupil's development. They enable teachers to specialize in a particular course which they teach year after year. Since the same courses are taught every year, they make it more practical to build up resources related to these courses, such as visual aids, resource books for teachers and pupils, teaching aids of various sorts.

Group graded lessons have such advantages as (1) they are reasonably well graded to pupil needs, without presenting the complex problems of close grading; (2) they make it possible to relate department worship closely to the class teaching; (3) they enable the workers in a department to share in planning their work; (4) departmental meetings for parents can be related to the teaching program; (5) observance of special days, missionary projects, and other departmental interests can be built right into the lesson materials; (6) visual aids can more easily be related to the curriculum by departments than if this has to be done for each class.

Those who prefer to use the uniform lessons do so for such reasons as (1) they stand in the long tradition of "international" lessons, with the same basic scripture selections used by all denominations, (2) they are best adapted for use in small churches which do not have the usual de-

77

partments and only a few classes, (3) they are more obviously centered in Bible study, (4) they make it easier to get substitute teachers, since the same basic scripture material is used throughout the church school, (5) they are easier to teach, (6) they are cheaper. In fairness to the reader, the author must say that he does not consider any of these arguments valid in determining the curriculum. Group graded materials are equally usable in most small churches, and closely graded materials can be adapted to situations which are not completely graded; both group graded and closely graded materials actually use more total Bible material than the uniform; teaching must be specifically related to the age of the pupils, and just because a person has read a lesson for the adult Bible class does not make him competent to substitute in a class of children; a slight difference in cost should not stand in the way of better Christian education. Moreover, it is impractical if not impossible to teach the same Bible material to all ages of pupils, and hence uniform lessons are not easier to teach effectively.

Most denominational publishers provide two systems of lessons from which local churches may choose—uniform and either group graded or closely graded. Graded materials are usually of higher educational quality, and should be favorably considered by committees on Christian education which are required to make the choice. A few denominations publish uniform lessons for adults only.

It is assumed by some that rural churches, because they are often smaller, can use uniform lessons more successfully than other types. Experience does not bear this out. A recent survey of rural churches situated in all parts of the country revealed that less than 25 percent are using uniform, 50 percent group graded, and over 25 percent closely graded lessons. Small schools can use group graded and graded materials, and their pupils are just as deserving of the best as those in larger schools.

4. *Presuppositions and Content.* The problem of choosing a system of curriculum materials for the church goes beyond that of deciding whether it shall be uniform, group graded, or closely graded. The available series also differ from each other in their underlying religious and educational outlook. That there should be such variety is inevitable, when we consider the differences in doctrine and polity among the denominations, the varieties of educational theory, and the wide range in size and educational outlook of the churches which must be served by the publishers.

(1) There is general agreement that the teaching of the Bible should have a large place in the curriculum, but there are different ways of using the Bible. Some hold that it is best to teach the Bible content as directly as possible, and let it do its own work with the pupil. Others feel that to be effective, the teaching of the Bible must be related to the interests and needs of the pupil of which he is already aware; only thus will it "speak to his condition." In practice, the first approach will usually mean beginning with the study of a Bible book or passage, and then through exposition and discussion relating it to present-day life. The second will more often begin with the consideration of some important life problem or some activity and go to the Bible as a source of inspiration and guidance. Its concern with life situations and activities other than Bible study may at first be confusing to those who are accustomed to the first approach.

(2) There is general agreement also that Christian ed-

ucation should result in commitment to Christ. But how is this best brought about? Some hold that this comes best through nurture—through the pupil's association with other Christians in the family and the church, and through Christian teachers who give witness to the faith, and interpret it by their teaching of the Bible, Christian beliefs, and Christian living. Others would add to this a more direct evangelistic appeal. This is a matter that goes deeper than method. It reaches to the very root of what it means to become a Christian, and how this re-birth comes about. It affects the whole curriculum.

(3) There is a vast difference also between series of lessons in their theological orientation and content. Theology is involved whenever religion is taught. Since most lay teachers are not competent theologians, they are dependent on their teaching materials for a consistent interpretation which is in harmony with the outlook of the church which they represent.

(4) In the matter of method, there are two major positions, with variations of all sorts between them. (a) The first holds that teaching is largely a matter of instructing the pupils in the established "truth" as found in the Bible and Christian doctrine. First he must learn the truth, then he will live it. (b) The second holds that true learning comes not so much from what the teacher does as from what the pupil does for himself. Learning comes through living, under guidance. Hence the emphasis on discussion, projects, and other kinds of activity.

The position on such problems which is adopted by a publisher of curriculum material will of course determine the type of material produced. In evaluating any curriculum series it is necessary first to find out the theory which underlies it. This can usually be done through a study of the prospectus or other booklets furnished by the publisher, followed by an examination of sample units of the material. For a church which holds one point of view to adopt material which embodies its opposite is to invite confusion and dissatisfaction. The material selected should either conform in general to the viewpoint of the church and its workers in which it is to be used, or the workers of that church should change their viewpoint through further study of what constitutes good Christian education.

This chapter has dealt with the meaning of curriculum, and the nature and purpose of published curriculum materials. It has emphasized that the choice of materials, and the nature of the curriculum which results from their use, are in the hands of the workers in the local church —the pastor, the director of Christian education, the committee on Christian education, the teachers and the officers. In the next chapter we will deal with the practical problems of curriculum selection and administration in the local church.

6 CURRICULUM ADMINISTRATION

The curriculum in any church consists of those influences and activities which are provided for the development of Christian discipleship. It is a home-made product, in which published materials have an important place, but only as they are creatively used to serve a purpose which is the church's own. This chapter will deal with the problems of developing an effective curriculum in the local church.

WHAT KIND OF CURRICULUM DO WE WANT?

To gain perspective, let us suppose that a church is "starting from scratch" to make a curriculum. This would be necessary in a new church, and it might happen in any church that wants to make a new approach to Christian education. Most churches are of course in the midst of an on-going program, but even they need to do some occasional re-thinking and evaluation of what they are doing.

82

This is primarily a job of the committee on Christian education. A careful study of the book *A Guide for a Curriculum in Christian Education,* published by the National Council of Churches, will be helpful.

In coming to its decision on the kind of curriculum that will best serve the church's needs, the committee will need to answer the following questions:

1. *What are our objectives?* Until the purpose is clear, there is no sound basis for curriculum. Statements of objectives which others have made can easily be found, but it is important that the workers in the local church give their own thought to the matter. In this book we have repeatedly used the simple but meaningful word *discipleship* as a statement of objective, with a brief interpretation of what it means on page 17. The following is a more elaborate statement:

> Christian education, by the initiative of God and the work of His Holy Spirit, has as its first object to guide the pupil to a knowledge and understanding of Divine revelation, and to bring him to a conscious acceptance of Christ as Master, Lord, and personal Savior. We believe that the pupil will come in this way (in accordance with his age) to repentance, to forgiveness of his sins and a new life full of faith, abnegation, and consecration to the service of his fellowmen.[1]

The committee on Christian education in one local church arrived at the following statement:

> Christianity is for us a faith, a fellowship, and a way of life —opened to us by Christ Jesus. The objectives of Christian education, therefore, are to encourage and to develop among persons, young and old:

---

[1] *Preparation of Curriculum Materials,* p. 10. World Council of Christian Education, New York.

1. A TRUST IN GOD AS OUR DIVINE FATHER, a habit of constant awareness of his presence, a questing for and a commitment to the Divine Purpose as disclosed in the orderly world and especially as revealed in Christ Jesus.

2. AN ACCEPTANCE OF CHRIST JESUS as the living expression of God's concern for humanity, as the ideal for human life, as an actual source of divine power for healing the human spirit and for realizing its destiny.

3. A KNOWLEDGE AND APPRECIATION OF THE CHRISTIAN COMMUNITY, beginning with its roots in Judaism, continuing in the founding of the primitive Church, including all Christlike men of whatever denomination since that time; a knowledge and appreciation of the history of that community, of its sacred writings, its sacraments, symbols, traditions, uses; skill in the techniques of private and public worship of God.

4. RESPONSIBLE MEMBERSHIP IN THE CHRISTIAN COMMUNITY— first, as members of this church; second, as members of the universal Church, the invisible fraternity of all Christlike men.

5. A COMMITMENT TO A WAY OF LIFE founded upon goodwill, appreciation of others, compassion, personal integrity. An expression of such a life in all our personal and social relations in today's world.

It is all too easy to make a statement of objectives that looks impressive, but then to forget it and proceed as if it did not exist. To be effective, objectives must be understood by the workers in the church school, and constantly used.

2. *How do we achieve our objectives?* The answer to this question involves a theory of Christian education. How can we work with our pupils so as to achieve our objectives? The basis for the discussion of this problem is to be found in the preceding chapter under the heading

"The Nature of Curriculum" (p. 68) and in the section "Presuppositions and Content" (p. 78).

Workers in the local church will need to come to their own conclusions concerning the points developed in these sections. They will need to answer such questions as: What place shall Bible teaching have in our curriculum? How shall we relate our pupils to the whole church? What place shall we give to evangelism, missions, social service, and so on? How can we best involve our families in the process of Christian education? What educational methods can we use most effectively?

3. *What are we now doing?* After it has been decided what the curriculum should be, a study should be made of what is now being done. Which of the agencies of Christian education are active in our church? What kind of program are they now carrying on? How are they contributing to our objectives?

With particular reference to the Sunday school, this study would try to get answers to such questions as: How are we organized by departments and classes? How good are our worship services? How well are our curriculum materials used? How effective is our teaching? How competent are our workers, and how faithful are they to their work? How is the morale (interest, discipline, attendance) of our pupils? What part are parents taking? What, really, are we succeeding in teaching?

4. *What improvements might we make?* Let us hope that this study of the present situation will reveal that good work is already being done. It will also reveal weaknesses which call for improvement in the curriculum. Perhaps the several agencies need to become more aware of what they can best contribute, or of better integration of their contributions. More stress may need to be put

on worship. It may be found that evangelism and missions are not having adequate attention. The relation of the church school to the whole church may need to be strengthened. The relation of the curriculum to the home may need to be developed. Teachers may need to be given a better understanding of their place in the curriculum.

CHOOSING CURRICULUM MATERIALS

It has been emphasized that to a large extent curriculum must be "home-made." However, lay workers do not have the time or the training and experience required to create their own teaching materials. They must depend on some form of published curriculum materials as a starting point for their own creative efforts.

The study of curriculum which we have suggested will therefore need to include an evaluation of the materials in use. If this leads to the conclusion that a change is desirable, a further study must be made to determine what materials might be selected better to serve the purpose.

1. *Criteria for Selection.* The basic question to be answered in evaluating the material in use, or other materials considered for adoption, is whether this series is the best that the church can use to achieve its purpose. This may require an examination of several series. Publishers will send a prospectus and sample materials on request. The committee making this study should seek answers to the following questions as a basis for reaching its conclusion (For a more detailed statement of criteria, see chapter 2 in *A Guide for Curriculum in Christian Education*):

(1) Is this series basically Christian in nature, and will it help us have the kind of Christian education that we need?

86

(2) Does it provide a comprehensive coverage of what is most important in Christian education, and are the several elements of content properly balanced so as to put emphasis on those things which are most vital?

(3) Is the treatment of the Bible—in amount of biblical material included, portions selected, and method of use— such as we want?

(4) Is the plan of grading (i.e., group or closely grading) such that we can best use it in our situation?

(5) Does it provide sufficiently for relation to the church so that we can make our Christian education a real part of the total church program?

(6) Does it include worship materials for the several departments, properly related to the teaching material?

(7) Does it take sufficient account of the abilities, interests, and needs of pupils so that its use will be a satisfying experience for them?

(8) Does it make provision for home relationships, in a way that is practical for us?

(9) Can our teachers handle these materials? Are they written so as to be easily understood? Are they helpful in biblical and theological interpretation? Are the methods suggested such as our teachers can use, or learn to use?

(10) Does it provide adequate and attractive material for pupils, such as text-books, reading books, workbooks, activity materials?

(11) Is the material attractive as to type size, page format, illustrations, use of color, binding?

(12) Is the cost of this series within the financial ability of our church to meet?

The last question, concerning cost, should not be allowed to weigh too heavily. The best quality materials are never the cheapest. Most churches do not spend enough rather than too much for curriculum materials. A yearly average expenditure of $3.00 to $4.00 per pupil should be considered a good investment. If this is beyond the present budget, it is time to increase the budget rather than to settle for cheap material.

Probably no system of curriculum materials will ever meet all these tests to the full satisfaction of any church. Considering the thousands of churches they must serve, it would be too much to expect denominational curriculum committees to produce materials which exactly please everybody. The nature of curriculum is such that printed materials must always be creatively adapted in actual use. If more workers realized this there would be less complaint about lesson materials.

2. *Shall we use a single series?* Our discussion thus far has assumed that a church will select a series of curriculum materials and use it throughout the church school. This is the most common practice. In most cases it is the wisest practice. A series is a unified whole, it "hangs together," with common objectives throughout, uniform theological and educational outlook, and builds in each age group on what has gone before. To mix up different series may lead to duplication and confusion. If effort is put on using a series effectively rather than on "shopping around" for something to substitute at one point or another the results are likely to be better.

There may be occasional unusual circumstances which make it wise to substitute another course in a given class or department, because everything considered this will better meet the abilities of teachers or the needs of pupils. In such cases, care should be taken that the substitution does not duplicate what is provided in the series before or after the point where the substitution is made, that it does not exclude something essential from the series, and that what is substituted is of a quality as high as or higher than what is replaced. A practice not to be encouraged is for individual teachers to select their own material to satisfy a peculiar interest or whim of their own.

Some churches with unusual educational leadership find it best to make their own curriculum by deciding first what they want to accomplish at each age and then selecting material from any source which will best serve their purpose. This involves problems which are beyond the purpose of this book.

3. *Why use denominational materials?* Theoretically, a church is free to choose any system of lesson materials which best suits its needs, no matter who publishes it. But there are important reasons why first consideration should be given to the publications of its own denomination.

(1) These materials are prepared with the needs of churches of that denomination in mind, by people who are within the traditions of the denomination, and responsible to the whole church for what they do.

(2) They are written from the viewpoint of the theology, history, church organization, and program of the denomination.

(3) They include the missionary and benevolent emphases of the denomination, and these are the local church's responsibility.

(4) As a member of the denomination, each church has an interest in what is done by its board of Christian education, and the board in turn has a right to expect the church's loyal support. Such support includes the duty of constructive criticism and suggestions for improvement.

(5) The problem of selecting curriculum material is

greatly simplified if only the series of a church's denomination need to be considered. It is then only a matter of choosing one of these series which best fits its needs. In most cases this should be the group graded or closely graded series.

In view of these considerations, it is strongly recommended that a church select its curriculum materials from the publications of its own denomination and concentrate its efforts on using them as effectively as possible. If a church finds it necessary to go outside its denomination, this should be done only in full knowledge of the disadvantages incurred, and with the expectation that such material will be supplemented with denominational materials for denominational emphases.

4. *What about "union" Sunday schools?* The foregoing discussion has assumed a Sunday school conducted by a single church affiliated with a denomination. What should be the policy respecting lesson materials of a Sunday school which is non-denominational or inter-denominational?

The principle still holds that such schools should use the materials best suited to their purpose. A non-denominational union school need not necessarily use the material of a non-denominational publisher. Denominational materials are not usually so sectarian as to be offensive to those of other denominations. It may even be better to learn something about the work of one denomination than to learn nothing at all about wider relationships and responsibilities.

Inter-denominational Sunday schools may well decide to use the material of one of the denominations which is party to the union, if this serves their needs best. Or they may decide to alternate the materials of the two or more denominations represented. In such case it is better to use the material of a given denomination for a cycle of three years, then that of another denomination for a similar period, than to alternate every year. It is better to use an entire series of one denomination at any given time than to mix things up by using some materials from each of the denominations. Supplementary material on church organization and missions may be secured from each of the other denominations. Thus the inter-denominational character of a Sunday school may be given positive value in ecumenical education, rather than allowing it to be an irritant.

USING CURRICULUM MATERIAL

The selection of a church school curriculum series is only the first step. This must be followed by education in its purpose, nature, and proper use. This is necessary not only for the workers in the church school, but also for parents and the church at large. Opportunities for such interpretation may be sought in any gathering of the church people, but particularly in women's and men's groups, parents' meetings, and workers' conferences. This is primarily the task of the general superintendent and department principals.

When a new series is being adopted, it is best to take several months for this process of education before the date of beginning its use. But it is a job which cannot be done once and for all. New people are constantly coming into the program, and others tend to forget what they once knew. Hence the need for continuing education. When new pupils are enrolled in the church school, a personal visit should be made to the parents with the purpose of interpreting the curriculum and showing them how they can cooperate in it.

The need for education in the nature and use of curriculum materials applies in particular to the workers in the program. No complaint is heard more frequently from teachers than that their lesson materials are not satisfactory. Usually the fault is not with the materials, but with the workers themselves, because they have not taken the trouble properly to understand and use them. Here are a few suggestions for training workers in the use of curriculum materials:

1. Include as many of them as possible in the study of materials which precedes selection of a particular series.

2. When a new series is adopted, hold one or more meetings for the purpose of studying the material in detail, so that every worker may become familiar with the whole as well as with the particular unit he is to teach.

3. At the beginning of the year, hold a retreat for workers, and devote a part of the program to a pre-view and interpretation of the curriculum for the year.

4. At the beginning of each quarter, have workers meet by departments to make a careful pre-view of their materials for the quarter.

5. When a new worker is appointed, hold a personal conference with him and explain the whole curriculum, as well as the particular unit which he is to teach.

6. Help workers with finding the resources, such as visual aids, which are needed in carrying out the teaching plans suggested.

7. Make it clear that the way a course is taught is the worker's own choice, for which the printed material serves as a resource. He should be its master, not its slave.

8. Insist on the importance of adequate preparation, so that the material may become the teacher's own, not just a hand-out of what someone else has said. There are

few problems which will not be solved by hard work and common sense.

ADMINISTRATIVE PROCEDURES

The mechanics of supplying workers with curriculum materials need to be established and understood by all workers. A principle to be followed is to make it as simple and easy as possible for workers to have the materials they need, so as to keep them free for the exacting job of teaching. A few suggestions follow:

1. Have one person place the orders for the entire church school, on the best estimate of needs that can be made from enrollment figures and teachers' requests. Use the order blanks supplied by the publisher.

2. Be sure to include in the order not only teachers' and pupils' books, but also pictures, activity sheets, audiovisuals, superintendent's manuals, parents' materials, and so on.

3. Place orders early, so that materials will arrive well before the opening of the quarter.

4. When the materials arrive, check them against invoices, and store in a convenient place until needed. Approve bills for payment promptly!

5. Deliver teachers' copies of materials to them as early as possible, so that they will have time to make adequate preparation for the next unit.

6. At the appropriate time, deliver materials for pupils to the teachers so that all pupils may be promptly supplied. Classes get out of hand if teachers have to spend time to hunt up material. Pupils lose interest if they are overlooked in the distribution.

7. Provide a convenient place, preferably a cabinet which can be locked, where teachers may keep pictures,

workbooks, and other materials which are not to be taken home.

8. Have a plan for return and storage of pictures, books, and other materials which are to be used in subsequent years. Much money is wasted on unnecessary new purchases if this provision is not made.

9. Make a preview each quarter of audio-visuals and other resources that will be required during the quarter so that orders may be placed early.

10. Establish a system for supplying workers with pencils, paper, crayons, scissors, maps, and other needed supplies. Failure to make resources and supplies available subjects teachers to trouble and expense, and usually impoverishes teaching because teachers will get on without them.

The following sections of this chapter will deal with some special problems, which are properly regarded as a part of the total curriculum.

AUDIO-VISUALS IN THE CURRICULUM

By audio-visuals we mean all those devices which help people to learn through seeing. They include such common aids to teaching as blackboards, charts, maps, posters, models, and printed pictures. They include also recordings, slides, filmstrips, and motion pictures, which require special equipment for their use.

Audio-visuals are increasingly being used in Christian education. This is happening because the newer types of audio-visuals are now readily available, and because of their undoubted effectiveness when properly used. Every good curriculum should include the use of this *seeing method* of teaching.

Printed pictures, especially for children, have long been a part of curriculum. The better curriculum materials now provide visual aids, with suggestions for their use included in the teaching plans. The audio-visuals appear on the order blank, along with the rest of the materials for the curriculum. They should by all means be used.

However, most audio-visual resources still exist apart from the published curriculum materials. Churches using them need to make their own selection and correlation. Workers should be aware of these vast resources for more effective teaching, and use them as extensively as feasible. Special attention must be given to this aspect of curriculum. The following suggestions may be helpful:

1. Have a sub-committee of the committee on Christian education take responsibility for encouraging and facilitating the use of audio-visuals.

2. Provide essential equipment for projection, perhaps beginning with a slide-filmstrip projector, record player, and portable screen, and install blinds for darkening one or more rooms. Add a movie projector, tape recorder, and opaque projector as this becomes possible.

3. Start a library of audio-visual materials, including a file of printed pictures, filmstrips recommended in the curriculum, slides and filmstrips of biblical subjects, and others which will be frequently used. Add to this library each year. Provide catalogs of audio-visual distributors from which selection can be made for rental.

4. Devote at least one meeting of the workers' conference to interpreting the meaning, value, and use of audio-visuals, with demonstrations of their use.

5. Include proposed expenditure for audio-visual equipment and materials in the annual budget for Christian education. Apart from expensive equipment and longer motion pictures, $50 to $100 per year will go a long way.

95

6. Suggest audio-visuals to teachers and department principals, through which they may make their work more effective.

7. Appoint one or more older boys as official projectionists, and train them in the use and care of equipment.

The effectiveness of audio-visuals depends on their proper use. When they are used in Christian education their purpose is not entertainment but aid to teaching. Therefore workers should first be clear on the purposes they wish to accomplish, then select a subject that will help achieve those purposes. Rarely should they just be shown to a class or department; rather make them an integral part of the teaching process, related to what has gone before and what comes after. To accomplish this, workers need to pre-view the subject in time to include it in the teaching plan.

This principle of effective use suggests that audio-visuals can best be used in the class session. However, this presents some difficulty when there are no separate classrooms.[2] In a group graded curriculum audio-visuals related to all the classes in a department may be shown in the department assembly, provided teachers are aware of what is to be shown and make proper use of it in their class sessions. In such case, the projection should be separate from the worship service unless the pictures are closely related to the worship theme. Usually it should occupy an additional period which is properly a part of class teaching rather than of worship. This is not impractical if the worship service on such occasions is made brief.

---

[2] See *How A Small Church Can Have Good Christian Education* by Virgil E. Foster, chapter 11, for excellent suggestions for use of audio-visuals in one-room churches and others with limited equipment. Harper & Brothers, 1956.

MISSIONS AND STEWARDSHIP

Education in missions and stewardship is an essential element of Christian education. Every good series of curriculum materials includes them, but special attention must be called to these emphases so that they will be properly taught, and what is included in the lesson materials needs to be enriched and given local application.

Even though missions and stewardship are included in curriculum material, they may not be effectively taught if teachers do not sense their importance. Teacher training should therefore include the meaning and significance of education in missions and stewardship, and guidance in the proper use of the material that is provided.

1. Missionary education may be enriched by use of the excellent materials prepared each year by the Friendship Press, which is an agency of the National Council of Churches. Each year this Press publishes reading books, pictures, teachers' guides, and visual aids for the theme of that particular year. These are distributed through the several denominational publishing houses. They do not replace the regular curriculum materials, but are supplemental to them. Some churches use them to good advantage in vacation church school.

Missions should be made specific by acquainting pupils with the missionary interests of their own church, and encouraging participation. In some cases, classes or departments may sponsor their own missionary projects. Audiovisuals are peculiarly effective in missionary education, and an abundance of such material is available.

Some churches find it helpful to have a sub-committee of the committee on Christian education for missionary education, which will work closely with the committee of the church which has responsibility for missions.

2. Stewardship applies to all of life, not just to the giving of money. As such, it is intimately related to the whole curriculum.

Stewardship education as applied to Christian giving is best related to the church school offering. This provides a concrete basis for such important teaching as:

(1) The meaning of Christian giving as an expression of Christian faith and life.

(2) The obligation and privilege of each church member to support his church through contributions to its budget.

(3) The causes in which the church is interested, as represented by the budget for items outside the support of its own work.

(4) Regular and systematic giving, through the use of weekly contribution envelopes.

Children and young people in the church school should not be overlooked in the annual canvass of the church. They should be helped to understand the needs of the church as represented in the budget, the causes in which the church is interested, and should have an opportunity to contribute to the church. Even younger children will enjoy bringing their offerings in envelopes, though they may not be asked to sign regular pledges until they are older.

In order that pupils may give to the church itself, and not just to the church school, all offerings should go to the church, while the church in turn makes provision in its budget for the support of the church school.

Here, as in so many things, the cooperation of parents is necessary in dealing with younger children. If the parents understand what is being attempted, they can help to interpret it to their children. One important consideration is for the pupils to have a sense of giving their own money, not just what parents put into their hands to carry to church. From a teaching standpoint, the significance of the church school offering is its value in teaching the meaning of Christian giving.

SPECIAL DAYS

Certain days, such as Thanksgiving, Christmas, and Easter, highlight the church school year. They are *special* because they have special significance in Christian experience and therefore deserve special attention in Christian education. Special day programs have a more important purpose than giving parents a chance to see their children perform.

Special days should be regarded as opportunities for Christian education. On the one hand, they take advantage of the pupils' interest in certain days and seasons such as Christmas and Easter. On the other hand, they channel this interest into the important Christian teachings which are bound up with these occasions. Special day programs which involve the whole church help to keep the church school an integral part of the church. The question of what days shall be observed and what kind of program shall be planned must be answered in terms of what will contribute most to Christian education.

1. *How can we make special days effective?*

(1) The occasions selected for observance, and the program planned, should be closely related to the objectives of the entire curriculum. They represent an opportunity to teach more effectively what in any case should be taught.

(2) Preparation for participation in songs, pageants, dramatizations, scripture reading, prayers, should be an educational experience for the pupils and not mere re-

99

50294

hearsal for a performance. If such preparation takes time away from more important matters, and puts an undue burden on teachers and pupils, it is a wrong use of special days.

(3) Programs for special days should be of high quality. It is probably better to do a few programs well than to try to observe every occasion that comes along.

(4) As far as possible, material for special day programs should grow out of the regular curriculum, so as to reinforce what is being taught. For example, a special program for Easter may utilize the hymns, stories, dramatizations, and other elements which have been a part of the curriculum for this season of the year. To turn aside for the learning of special program material, which in many cases is inferior in quality, is to waste valuable time.

(5) Through the special day program, the participants and the congregation should "get inside" of the true meaning of the day which is celebrated, not just render or enjoy a performance.

(6) Some special days can best be observed in each department, rather than by a general public service. Parents may be invited for such occasions.

(7) The training of workers is essential to effective observance of special days. They must help carry the spirit of the occasion to their pupils.

(8) The cost of special day celebrations must be carefully weighed against the possible values. We have referred to the cost in time and interruptions of regular work. Sometimes they are also costly in goodwill because they arouse attitudes of false pride and jealousies.

2. *What special days or seasons should be observed?* The high seasons of the church year should of course be included, such as Thanksgiving, Advent and Christmas,

Passion Week and Easter, and Whitsunday or Pentecost (marking the birth of the church). Certain other occasions represent good educational opportunities. The list that follows includes only a few representative examples.

(1) *Thanksgiving.* The emphasis should be on gratitude for God's providence. Gratitude may be expressed in some kind of service project. Thanksgiving has become so secularized as a day for football and big dinners that if the church can do even a little to re-establish its original religious significance, it will be worth the effort.

(2) *Christmas.* Celebration of Christmas may extend over several weeks. It should be a reminder of God's grace in giving us the Christ Child and emphasize goodwill among men. It is a time of giving and receiving, but the receiving attitude should not overshadow the joy of Christian giving. It is a time for effective use of music peculiar to the season. It should include projects for the home. A church program in the nature of a family celebration in which all participate is better than an entertainment presented by the children.

(3) *Easter.* The message of Lent and Easter is that of Christ's suffering, death, and triumphant resurrection. Probably no aspect of Christian teaching gives teachers more trouble than this. Preparation should therefore include an opportunity for workers to understand the meaning of these great events in Christian history. Teachers of children especially need help in handling the message of Easter. Easter may be a time of the singing of birds and the return of the grass and flowers, but if it is no more than this it falls short of the Christian gospel. Easter presents opportunities for many types of special programs, such as Good Friday services, sunrise services, whole-family church services, first communion for those just coming

into full membership, plays and pageants, but should never be an occasion for mere entertainment. Easter can probably be observed better through what is done in and by classes and departments than through programs prepared for the whole church.

(4) *Mother's Day* has been so commercialized by vendors of flowers and candy, and so sentimentalized by churches, that many good mothers would rather have nothing to do with it. However, when Mother's Day is transformed into an opportunity to exalt the Christian home, it regains real significance. A good way to celebrate this occasion is to have a family worship service for the whole church.

(5) *National Family Week,* scheduled for the first two Sundays of May and the week lying between, is observed in many churches as an opportunity to emphasize the Christian family. Mother's Day is absorbed in this as the final Sunday, and is thus put in proper perspective.

(6) *Children's Day,* usually the second Sunday in June, was originally an occasion for having children present an entertainment for the enjoyment of parents and friends. Some fantastic programs were presented which had little relation to Christian education. In recent years many churches have changed the character of this day in more desirable directions.

As *church school day* it is an occasion to bring to the whole church its responsibility for Christian education, and to acquaint the church with what is being done in the church school.

Indicative of this changing character of Children's Day is the action of the Methodist Church in making it the first Sunday of National Family Week, specifying that its purpose shall be to emphasize the "responsibility of the church for our children," and annually preparing a printed program for the guidance of churches in observing it.

As *commencement day* for churches which have a summer recess for the church school, this occasion can be used for presenting some of the accomplishments of the year's work in program and exhibits, promoting pupils, and presenting Bibles. It may be scheduled earlier or later than the second Sunday in June to correspond with the closing date of the church school.

The most effective program for these purposes is one which grows out of the work of the year, not one which comes from outside sources and requires a lot of time for rehearsals. Younger departments may sing some of their songs which they love best. Dramatizations which have been most successful may be brushed up and repeated. Older pupils may give talks on subjects with which they have been dealing, and help in leading the worship service. The pastor may preach a brief sermon. The occasion should be one for worship and enlightenment, not mere entertainment. It is appropriate for this to be done in the morning worship service of the church, though some prefer to make it a special service at another hour. If the attendance is too large for the size of the church sanctuary, it is desirable to have two services, one for younger and the other for older pupils. Since this is an occasion for all ages, the term "children's day" had best be avoided.

(7) *Christian Education Week,* in early fall, centers the attention of the church and community on the importance of Christian education. It may include such events as rally day, consecration of workers, parent-worker meetings, training sessions for workers, and general community meetings.

(8) *National Holidays,* such as Washington's Birthday

and Independence Day, may have a place in the church school calendar of special days *provided* they help to teach the implications of the Christian faith for citizenship and patriotism. Otherwise they had best be left to secular celebrations.

Where may program material be found? It has already been suggested that this may be drawn largely from the regular curriculum. Usually there are helpful suggestions for special days in the church school literature. Printed program suggestions are usually also available from denominational headquarters. The best programs are homemade, and even if a prepared program is used it should be adapted to the church's own situation.

7 THE CURRICULUM OF WORSHIP

Worship is one of the most important elements in the curriculum of Christian education. In support of this statement, consider the following propositions:

1. Worship is at the heart of what the church is and does. The church is the only institution which regularly brings people together for communion with God, provides buildings and equipment for this purpose, trains and employs men to lead congregations in this experience. Without worship, it would not be a church at all.

2. Worship, whether private or congregational, is a natural expression of the human spirit. The desire for communion with God is as basic and real as the desire for food and drink and any other value which gives life meaning. This is true for the young child as well as for the mature man or woman.

3. While the impulse to worship is deep-seated and natural, the expression of this impulse in the act of Chris-

tian worship must be learned. Education in worship includes an understanding of the nature of God who is worshiped, man's relation to God, the forms through which congregational worship is realized through an order of worship, the materials of worship such as hymns, prayers, responses, and the proper attitude in worship. Christian education which seeks to bring persons into the faith and life of the church cannot neglect experience and training in worship.

4. More than anything else we teach in the church school, education in worship can be related to actual experience. This experience exists in the worshiping congregation to which the learner should be related, and the activity of worship in department and class. The meaning of Christian worship, the forms and materials of worship, and proper conduct in worship are best taught in relation to actual participation in worship.

THE MEANING OF WORSHIP

Before we can profitably consider the place and practice of worship in the church school, we must come to some understanding of what is meant by worship. Worship is communion with God. It is a personal approach to God, in which the worshiper experiences God's response to the human creature. It is active seeking for the presence of God as well as response to him. "In worship, faith, hope and love come to fruition in an experience of God."[1]

A *service of worship* provides an opportunity for leader and congregation to experience worship. The particular type of the service will vary with the age of the worshipers, but should always include those elements which give expression to the genuine attitude of worship. Randolph

---

[1] Barclay, W. C., *The Church and a Christian Society*, p. 198.

Crump Miller has described the complete act of worship as follows:

> First, we praise and adore God for his majesty and his glory. Then we express our sense of separation from God and our fellows as our self-will sets up a barrier to true fellowship, and this is our confession of sin. There is the discovery of God's will for us as we listen to the Scriptures and sermon. We express our common faith in the God of Jesus Christ, state our deepest needs and desires for ourselves and others, and thank God for all our blessings. We offer ourselves and our possessions to God. Worship closes with the assurance that God will continue to bless us in all our doings.[2]

Obviously the mere presence of a person in a service of worship, even though he joins in the hymns, responses, recital of prayers, and offering, and listens to the reading of the Word and the sermon, does not assure that he will be a worshiper. Worship is an experience of the soul which depends on the meeting of the worshiper with God. A proper order of worship is conducive to this experience. So also is the atmosphere created by the leader and other participants, and the character of the room in which worship is conducted.

By this standard, much of what is called worship in the church school is not worship at all. In many cases the service is haphazard, the pupils not in the right attitude, and the room inappropriate. Some leaders are more concerned with an interesting program than with a service that leads to worship. A great transformation could take place in many church schools if primary attention were given to the development of worship, and the training of leaders of worship.

---

[2] Miller, R. C., *Education for Christian Living*, p. 244. Prentice-Hall, 1956.

PARTICIPATION IN WORSHIP

Basic to all education in worship is the experience of participation in worship. The curriculum rightly includes worship as one of its major elements.

1. *Participation in the Worshiping Congregation.* The high moment in the life of the church comes when the whole congregation is together seeking communion with God. No person because of his youth should be deprived of this experience. To be sure, this presents problems. Church services are not usually planned with children in mind. They seem unduly long for children, especially the sermon. Mere presence in the service does not assure that the children will worship, and some feel that their restless presence even detracts from worship for others. Yet Christian education is so concerned with "education for the sanctuary" that some way must be found for inclusion of the experience of church worship. There are several ways in which this has been worked out:

(1) In some churches it is the custom for whole families to attend worship, and it might be added, for all to go to Sunday school. Here there is no problem, except that of devising a service which is an adequate expression of worship for all ages.

(2) Some churches make provision for participation of younger members in the first part of the service only, either regularly or occasionally. The problem of orderly withdrawal of the children at the appointed time can usually be worked out by having them go while the congregation is standing for a hymn. It is best for families to come together and sit as family groups, though sometimes children are brought as department or class groups. There may be a children's story or sermon, but this is not essential. Instruction in the meaning of the service should be

given, either by the pastor at an appropriate point in the service (adults can profit from this, too!), or in department and class groups. Some activity must be provided for children after they leave the service. This may be the regular class session for these children, or an additional opportunity for Christian education.

(3) Other churches have an occasional service for the whole family, with proper recognition of the presence of younger members, both in content and length of the service. This may be done on Rally Day, Christmas, Easter, and Childrens' Day, but does not need to be limited to special days. It is an art to plan a service that has meaning and value for both young and old, but many pastors are doing it successfully. Not everything needs to be on the plane of children. They have the capacity to "stretch up" toward more mature understanding. Moreover, there are overtones of value in the service, such as reverent atmosphere, music, and sense of participation, which do not depend on understanding all the words that are spoken.

(4) A few churches have ventured into having a weekly family service, which is a part of the whole educational program. This does not take the place of the regular congregational service of worship. It is usually held at the beginning of the church school, followed by a full hour of department and class activity, including study groups for parents and other adults. It is a brief service of 15 to 25 minutes, and is held in the sanctuary with the pastor in charge. It is a *church* service, with a simplified order of worship, and a brief story or sermon, which at times may be related to what is to follow in classes. Adults who feel that they are deprived of a sermon directed to them can also attend the regular church service, which comes at a later hour.

There is no one plan that can be called best. So much depends on numbers, seating capacity of the sanctuary, availability of rooms where activity can go on during part of the church service, and the ability of the pastor to minister to children. It is usually more easily worked out in small churches than in large. Workers responsible for Christian education can find some workable plan once they sense the importance of participation in congregational worship. The pastor's cooperation is essential, and pains should be taken to make clear to the congregation the reasons for any new plan that is undertaken.

2. *Departmental Worship.* Whatever plan for participation in the general worship of the church may be worked out, it is proper also to have worship as a part of the church school program. This may be by individual departments, some combination of departments, or for the school as a whole. Worship in the departments of the church school has values and provides opportunities which make it an important part of the curriculum.

(1) It recognizes worship as a normal part of Christian experience, and a proper activity when Christians gather together.

(2) It makes it possible to relate worship to the age and experience of pupils, through the use of hymns, prayers, stories and other materials which are within their understanding. Worship should be spontaneous and natural, coming out of and leading back into daily relationships.

(3) It provides opportunity for training in the meaning and materials of worship, in close relation to the experience itself.

(4) It enables workers to inter-relate worship and the teaching program, for the benefit of both.

(5) It gives opportunity for pupils to participate in the planning and conduct of worship.

(6) It helps to prepare pupils for participation in the general worship of the church.

3. *How should pupils be grouped for worship?* The usual plan is to follow the departmental groupings which have been given earlier. However, there are few churches which have either the numbers or the necessary rooms for such complete grading. Hence some combinations need to be made. As a general rule, the younger the pupils, the more they need to be grouped with others of their own age. Younger departments should therefore be given the advantage in the use of limited facilities. If there is a room in addition to the church sanctuary, the older departments may be combined for worship in the sanctuary, and the younger children use the additional room. Every effort should be made to give younger children an experience of worship of their own, even if it requires curtaining or screening a corner for them, or having them come at a different hour.

There still remains the problem of some churches that have just one room in which all must worship together if there is to be group worship at all. How are hymns, scripture, story, talk, and other parts of the service to be chosen to meet the needs of all? No doubt there are some familiar hymns, an occasional story or audio-visual, as well as scripture readings and prayers which will have some appeal to all. Beyond this, it is good practice to include some elements in the program which have a particular appeal to one or another of the age-groups represented, such as a children's hymn or story, a short talk aimed especially at young people, and something which gives adults an experience on their level. Opportunity for participation, such as receiving the offering and taking a part in the service, can also be passed around. This is not very different from the problem in a family where there are various ages of children present. The more mature can be taught to practice forbearance so that children may have their "inning," and children are accustomed to long-suffering in the presence of young people and adults.

There may be value in such a whole-school service of worship, yet it has few of the values listed above for departmental worship. We would urge leaders in one-room churches to consider working out some plan which combines the congregational worship of the church with worship in the church school. Participation in the regular church service, or a family service, under the leadership of the pastor, is likely to prove more effective than a general church school assembly, which too easily degenerates into a kind of entertainment or pep meeting. We would especially urge this last point against a regular general assembly for the whole church school where departmental worship is possible.

4. *Should worship precede or follow classes?* Some prefer to have worship first so that pupils will come to it unfatigued, and may be led to approach class sessions in a proper spirit. Others prefer to have classes first so that teachers may begin their work as soon as the first pupils arrive, and so that teaching may help prepare for the worship that follows. Either plan seems to work out satisfactorily. In case two departments need to use the same chapel, one must have worship before classes and the other after.

When worship is conducted before class sessions, there is no need to have a closing service. Pupils may be dismissed from classes when the signal for closing is given.

Closing "exercises" serve no useful purpose, and they take up time that is needed for teaching. An exception to this may be allowed when all classes meet in the same room and no time is consumed in re-assembling them. Even in such cases, it is to be questioned whether the time could not be used to better purpose by the teachers. Review of the lesson by the superintendent is not practical when graded materials are used, and was never of much value. Reports on attendance can be posted on a bulletin board if this is of any interest to the pupils.

CHARACTER AND QUALITY OF WORSHIP

1. *Type of Service.* The type of service which is appropriate depends on the age of pupils in the department. For pre-school children, worship is a normal and integral part of the whole church school session, without their being taken to a different room for a formal service. Brief moments of worship may be planned to come at almost any point in the session.

For primary and junior departments, two types of worship are practiced, each with its own values.

(1) The usual procedure is to have pupils assemble as a department, with a more or less formal service. When well planned, such a service is attractive to children, and can be good training in congregational worship.

(2) The alternative procedure is to make worship a part of the class session, as with pre-school children, so that the work of the whole session may be properly integrated under a single leader. Under this plan there is no department assembly, but usually classes are larger, with a head teacher and one or more assistants. In both cases pupils may be given an opportunity to share in the planning and leadership of the service.

Junior high and senior high school departments will usually have a departmental worship service in the Sunday school, though some churches prefer to give the whole time to class work, encourage these pupils to attend the general church service, and meet their graded worship needs in the evening fellowship groups. Older young people and adults may be presumed to have their worship needs met by attendance at the general church service, so that their full time may be given to class sessions. If they have worship in the church school, it should be brief and informal.

As pupils become more mature, they can have a larger part in planning and conducting their own services. However, this should never be an excuse for accepting less than thorough preparation, high quality, and dignity.

2. *Quality of the Service.* What should be true of all Christian education is especially true of worship: nothing but the best is good enough. The purpose of worship in the church school that has been detailed above is not achieved in many church schools because services are poorly conceived and badly conducted, in rooms which are inappropriate, and with pupils whose attitude is the very opposite of worshipful.

After an extensive study of the subject, Professor Helen Edick has said:

> The quality of children's worship is highest when children are comfortable physically and mentally, when they have been prepared for the experience, when they understand something of the purpose of the service, when the structure is stable, the service short, and when materials are familiar and understandable.[3]

---

[3] *Religious Education*, Vol. 50, No. 3, p. 173.

A good service of worship has the following qualities:

(1) It is *directed to God,* and gives the worshiper an opportunity for communion with God. It is not aimed at entertainment.

(2) It is *Christian,* with hymns, prayers, story, and other elements selected for their contribution to our highest conception of God in Christ.

(3) It is *serious in purpose,* seriously conducted by the leaders, and elicits a serious attitude in the congregation.

(4) It has *reality.* It is not a mere mouthing of words, but an experience of the soul in communion with God.

(5) It has *unity,* with materials selected so as to emphasize a central theme, to which hymns, scripture, prayers, and story contribute.

(6) It has *movement,* both in moving along in an orderly manner without interruptions, and ascending toward a climax in re-dedication to God. (Read again the quotation from R. C. Miller on page 107.)

(7) It has *rhythm,* which is achieved through use of responses between leader and congregation, and through directing attention now to man and his need, and again to God and his power to supply that need.

(8) There is *participation* by the congregation—outwardly in singing, responses, and offering, and inwardly in sharing in the thought of the scripture, prayers and sermon.

(9) It is preceded by *preparation,* both of the leader so that he may come with thorough familiarity with what is to be done and a quiet and devotional frame of mind, and of the congregation so that they may approach worship in quiet anticipation of God's presence and blessing.

LEADERSHIP OF WORSHIP

When the whole church school meets together for worship, or when there is a "main school" consisting of a combination of the older departments, it is customary for the general superintendent to serve as the leader of worship. However, this is not necessarily a part of his job. It is more important that he provide good leadership than that he take the responsibility himself. Some superintendents can lead worship acceptably, while some will do better to appoint other leaders who are better qualified. The pastor, who is trained for worship leadership, should have a part in church school worship.

In graded church schools, the department principals are usually responsible for leading worship. They in turn may get others to help them, pupils, teachers, the superintendent, or the pastor.

Leading a congregation into an experience of worship is an art. It requires an understanding of the meaning and purpose of worship. It requires a great deal of advance preparation. It requires an awareness of spiritual reality and quiet reverence which may be reflected in the congregation. It requires self-effacement so that attention may be directed to God, and not to the leader. It requires a sense of appropriateness and timing, so that just the right directions will be given when needed, and no more than needed. In short, leaders of worship need to be trained for their work.

Should pupils have a part in planning and conducting worship? The usual answer is *yes*. There are various ways in which they may participate. There may be a department committee which works with the principal in planning the service, or again a teacher and class may plan for a given Sunday. Pupils may conduct the service, or take such parts in it as reading the scripture, leading the prayer, making a talk or telling a story, giving a dramatization, or making some other contribution. They may prepare the room before the service, act as ushers, and collect the offering. The age of pupils will determine the part they can take, but some pupil leadership is possible in all departments.

In favor of this practice it is to be said that (1) pupils take more interest when they have a part; (2) they learn something about the meaning of worship if they have proper guidance in planning and preparing to participate; (3) they may help bring the service more nearly into the experience of others of their own age; (4) the testimony of their own comrades may be more effective with pupils than that of adults; (5) it prepares pupils for future leadership.

Against the practice it may be argued that (1) it may lead to a lower quality of worship service; (2) it may increase the tendency to make it a "program" rather than an experience of worship; (3) it may reduce the dignity of the occasion; (4) it may have a tendency to obtrude the leadership on the congregation, rather than effacing it in favor of attention on worship; (5) it is confusing to have several persons participate in the same service, particularly if it is not done with ease and grace.

These values are real. The dangers are no less real, but may be overcome to an extent by careful training and guidance. We would conclude that the leadership of worship is primarily an adult's job, but he may associate pupils with himself from time to time. Always they should be thoroughly trained in what they are to do, and have its seriousness impressed on them. Opportunities for leadership should not be given just to those who are "good at it," but should be extended to others so that they too may share and learn.

THE ORDER OF SERVICE

The order of service is the arrangement of what is to be done by leaders and pupils, so that the experience of worship may result. Simplicity and brevity are good characteristics for an order of service, especially for children. The elements usually included are:

1. *Musical prelude,* to help create an atmosphere of quiet reverence in anticipation of worship. At times the prelude may consist of the music of a hymn which is to follow, to help establish the tune.

2. *Call to worship, call to prayer, offering sentences, benediction*—these may often be simple scripture verses, or brief verses of song. They may be in the form of a statement by the leader and a response by the pupils. Such responses can be quickly memorized, or a copy of the order of service containing them may be handed to the pupils.

3. *Hymns,* selected for their appropriateness for worship and in harmony with the theme of the service. They should be Christian in sentiment. The words should be good poetry. The music should be appropriate to the sentiment of the words, and within the capacity of the pupils to sing. Hymns must be within the range of the pupil's experience and understanding. If a good hymnbook is used, one that has been prepared for the department in question, most of the hymns will be suitable for that age. Some hymns require all the verses to give their complete message, hence verses should not be omitted at random. Needless to say, a good accompanist is essential.

4. *Prayers.* This is the hardest part for most leaders, yet prayer is at the very heart of worship. The leader must put into words what should be in the minds and hearts of the congregation. Avoid vain repetitions, meaningless words, and a sanctimonious voice. Be natural and sincere, and be sure that you are yourself speaking to God. Never use prayer as an indirect means of teaching or admonishing the pupils. Use simple words that are understood by the pupils. If you are uncertain of yourself, think out carefully what you are going to say, and write it down. If you use a prayer that someone else has written, be sure you make it your own by carefully thinking it through beforehand.

5. *Scripture.* An appropriate scripture reading, or a responsive reading, may be included, but this is not essential. First be sure that it serves a purpose in the service. Sometimes the scripture can be combined with the story or other message. Sometimes the reading may be an appropriate poem or other selection.

6. *A story or talk,* which emphasizes and interprets the theme of the service, serves the same purpose as the sermon in church worship. Stories must be carefully selected for their contribution to worship, and so well prepared that they can be freely and fluently told. If a talk or sermon is to be used, it must of course be of appropriate length for the age of the congregation, deal with matters they can understand and appreciate, and be given in simple and direct language. An audio-visual may at times take the place of story or talk, but must be selected with great care for its contribution to worship.

7. *Offering.* The offering is properly a part of worship. It gives an opportunity for response to God in the giving of substance. In younger departments it may be

confusing to collect the offering during worship because the children have trouble finding their contribution when the plate is passed. This may be avoided in one of two ways: (1) have the pupils place their offerings in baskets at the door as they enter, and at the time of the offering have appointed "deacons" bring the baskets forward; (2) if classes precede worship, have each class collect its own offering, and a class representative present it in worship. The use of offering envelopes is highly recommended.

The particular way in which these elements are combined in a service of worship depends on the leader's sense of how worship will best be achieved. As has already been suggested, in pre-school departments there is no formal worship service, but any of the above elements may be used in the course of the session.

A service for the primary group should not be more than 10 to 20 minutes in duration. The order of service might be as follows:

> Musical prelude
> Call to worship
> Lord's prayer, or some other unison prayer
> Hymn
> Scripture and/or story or talk
> Prayer by the leader
> Offering:
>> Offering Response and/or prayer, spoken or sung
> Hymn
> Benediction
> Musical postlude

A junior department may have a somewhat more elaborate service, but 15 to 20 minutes should still be maximum length. As an example, we will reproduce herewith an order of service which was mimeographed on a single sheet 5½ inches by 8½ inches.

This order was used for six or eight weeks, thus allowing pupils to become familiar with it, and then was changed to prevent the monotony of sameness. Each Sunday the hymns, scripture, story or talk, and the content of the prayer were selected to suit the theme, and thus provide variety. For example, for the theme "Courage to Stand for Christian Convictions," the story of Stephen might be used, introduced by the single verse Acts 6:8. The story might be told, or presented through use of the sound filmstrip which is available. Appropriate hymns would be "Dare to Be Brave" and "Forward Through the Ages," which would be taught to the pupils in a training period prior to this service. The prayer could emphasize thanking God for our Christian leaders like Stephen, and asking God to give us courage to be true to our convictions.

ORDER OF WORSHIP

Prelude *(with lighting of the candles)*

*Call to Worship

    Leader: I was glad when they said unto me,
             Let us go into the house of the Lord.

    People: Whatever we do in word or deed, let us do in the name of the Lord Jesus, giving thanks to God the Father through him.

    All
     sing: Holy, Holy, Holy! Lord God Almighty!
            Early in the morning our song shall rise to thee.
            Holy, Holy, Holy, Merciful and Mighty!
            Perfect in power, in love and purity. Amen.

The Lord's Prayer

*HYMN

OFFERING

Call to Giving

Leader: Because we love thee and thy work,
          Our offering now we make;

People: Be pleased to use it as thine own,
          We ask for Jesus' sake.

*When the offering is presented, all sing:
          All things come from thee, O Lord;
          And of thine own have we given thee. Amen.

SCRIPTURE AND STORY OR TALK

PRAYER (by the leader)

Response
          Hear our prayer, O Lord;
          Hear our prayer, O Lord;
          Incline thine ear to us,
          And grant us thy peace. Amen.

HYMN

BENEDICTION

All repeat:
          May the words that we say,
          And the thoughts that we pray,
          Stay with us and help us,
          Our Father, today. Amen.

POSTLUDE (with extinguishing of the candles)

(* All stand.)

The following service was used for the period from
Easter to Pentecost in a junior high school department, the
only variation being the prelude and postlude, the hymns,
the scripture, and meditation. This was mimeographed as
a four-page 5½ x 8½ folder, the service itself occupying
the two inside pages.

ORDER OF WORSHIP

THE NOTICES

* * *

LIGHTING OF THE CANDLES

RESPONSIVE CALL TO WORSHIP *(standing)*

    Leader: Christ the Lord is risen!
    People: He is risen indeed!
    Leader: Sing unto the Lord!
    People: For he has done excellent things!
    Leader: Sing, O heavens; and be joyful, O earth!
    People: For the Lord has comforted his people.
    Leader: Thanks be to God!
    People: For he has given us the victory!

HYMN TO CHRIST

UNISON PRAYER OF INVOCATION *(seated)*

O God of Peace, who hast taught us that in returning and rest we shall be saved, in quietness and confidence shall be our strength; hear us and forgive us, so that in receiving thy strength and forgiveness, we may be enabled to worship and serve thee more fully; in the name of our Lord Jesus Christ. Amen.

PRAYER OF INTERCESSION *(to be said by the leader, with silence following each thought during which the congregation prays silently.)*

Hear us, O God, and look in pity upon our many necessities, since thou alone art able to satisfy all our desires. Especially do we commend to thy holy keeping:

    All who today are far from home and friends:
    All who today must go hungry or cold:
    All who suffer pain and injury:
    All who are filled with anxiety or loneliness:
    All who are facing danger:
    All who must work or keep watch while others rest:

Give to them all, we pray, such a sense of thy presence

with them as may turn their loneliness into comfort and their trouble into peace, through Jesus Christ. Amen.

LORD'S PRAYER

HYMN

THE WORD OF GOD

"The Lord hath more truth and light to break forth out of his Holy Word."—John Robinson

OLD TESTAMENT LESSON

NEW TESTAMENT LESSON

MEDITATION

THE MORNING OFFERING

DOXOLOGY

PRAYER OF DEDICATION

RESPONSIVE READING *(standing)*

Leader: Have this mind among yourselves, which you have in Christ Jesus,

People: Who, though he was in the form of God, did not count equality with God a thing to be grasped,

Leader: But emptied himself taking the form of a servant,

People: Being born in the likeness of men.

Leader: And being found in human form he humbled himself, and became obedient unto death,

People: Even death on a cross.

Leader: Therefore God has highly exalted him and bestowed on him

People: The Name which is above every name,

Leader: That at the name of Jesus every knee should bow, in heaven and on earth and under the earth,

Unison: And every tongue confess that Jesus Christ is Lord, to the glory of God the Father.

HYMN All hail the power of Jesus' name!
Let angels prostrate fall;
Bring forth the royal diadem,

124

And crown him Lord of all,
Bring forth the royal diadem,
And crown him Lord of all.   Amen.

UNISON BENEDICTION *(seated)*

Now may the God of peace who brought again from the
dead our Lord Jesus, the great shepherd of the sheep, by
the blood of the eternal covenant, equip you with everything good that you may do his will, working in you that
which is pleasing in his sight, through Jesus Christ, to
whom be glory forever and ever.   Amen.

These are but examples, from which many variations
are possible. It is wise to use a given order for a period of
weeks so that pupils may become familiar with it. For
pupils who are able to read, the program may be written on
a blackboard or large card, or mimeographed so that each
may have his own copy. This allows the leader to use unison prayers and responses without their having to be memorized in advance. For junior pupils, it is best to limit the
mimeographed program to a single sheet no larger than
the hymnbook. They may be kept in the front of the
hymnal for ease of distribution and collection. Explain to
the pupils that they are to be used on successive Sundays
and should therefore be carefully handled. Any temptation to convert the sheets into gliders should be curbed
at once!

WHERE TO GET SUGGESTIONS

The worship service must be the leader's own, though
perhaps prepared with the aid of a pupil committee. It is
folly to expect that such services can be packaged by someone else, so that all the leader has to do is to use them
unchanged. Such prepared services are rarely satisfactory
for any given local situation. Yet they may be helpful in

getting the leader started on making his own service, and often the stories, hymns, and other materials they suggest can be used.

The worship suggestions that are included in curriculum materials and in denominational workers' magazines are readily available to leaders. *The International Journal of Religious Education* has suggested programs for each of the departments. The church library should provide books of worship suggestions and resources, including selected stories, pictures, responses, and so on.

It cannot be too strongly emphasized, however, that all such helps are but resources to which leaders of worship may turn for suggestions and materials. Effective worship will not result until they do the necessary work to create services which are fitted to their understanding of the worship needs of the groups they lead.

THE WORSHIP ROOM

Environment is important in creating the right atmosphere for worship. Care should be given to having worship groups meet in rooms that are appropriate for worship.

The church sanctuary is the one place that has been built and equipped for the sole purpose of worship. It is unfortunate that so many church schools are not permitted to use the sanctuary, or by preference of the leaders do not use it. There are reasons why the sanctuary will not be used regularly by young children, such as its size and adult seating equipment, but even young children should have an occasional experience of worship in the sanctuary. Older groups may well use it as a regular meeting place.

Some churches have provided a smaller chapel in addition to the sanctuary. When the pews and chancel furniture are of appropriate size for younger worshipers, it may be used in rotation by two or more departments each Sunday.

Most departments need to use some other room than the sanctuary or a chapel. Such rooms should be made as congenial to worship as possible, even though they may be used for other purposes at other times. Some type of chancel effect (worship center) may be set up when worship is to take place, and removed at other times. Let this be done with care and in good taste. Some so-called worship centers we have seen are not aids but deterrents to worship. If possible, the seating should be arranged as in church, with a center aisle. Ideally, the length of the room should be twice its width. As a matter of course, it should be kept meticulously clean and orderly. Let it be granted that most church schools have to do the best they can with conditions which are far from ideal, but this is no excuse for not exercising imagination and ingenuity in making the best use of what they have.

When worship is a part of class activity, as with younger children, the arrangement of the room may be informal and more home-like than church-like. But even classes may have an accustomed plan for arrangement and seating, and may use a simple worship center.

TRAINING IN WORSHIP

The basis of all training in worship is the experience of worship. But the experience is in turn dependent on learning the nature and meaning of worship, as well as the forms and materials that are used in worship services.

1. In the broadest sense, the whole curriculum contributes to worship. Learning about God and his disposition toward man; learning about man and his dependence on God; study of the Bible; lesson units and courses on wor-

ship—all these are included in a good curriculum, and should help pupils in understanding and participating in worship.

2. More specifically, instruction may be given in relation to the worship service itself. Pupils should learn what it means to worship, the purpose of the several elements in a service of worship, the meaning of Christian symbols, how to conduct themselves during worship, and how to achieve communion with God. Pupils should learn that to worship means more than just being quiet and listening to what someone else has to say; they must be active in the process of seeking communion with God. Opportunity for this kind of teaching is greatly increased when pupils participate in the worship of the whole congregation.

3. The materials used in worship must be taught if worship is to be facilitated. Pupils need to learn the meaning of hymns as well as how to sing them properly, they need to learn prayers and other responses, they need to learn to listen for the message of the story or sermon.

The complaint is frequently heard that the singing in worship services is poor. If this means that pupils do not sing loud and lustily, perhaps it is better so. Participation in singing is a necessary part of worship, but it should be from the heart, with appreciation of the words and the music. Training in understanding and proper use of hymns will usually overcome any difficulty with this problem. It is better for pupils to know and love a few good hymns, and expand their repertoire as rapidly as possible, than to expect them to sing anything in the hymnbook. The leader may at times bring to his aid someone who is especially competent in teaching hymns, but this should not interfere with worship itself.

The question is properly raised how this kind of instruction can be given without making the worship service a mixture of teaching and worship, with perhaps no worship at all resulting. We are not advocating interspersing worship with exhortation and instruction. There is a simple way of handling this problem. The department assembly time may be used in part for worship and in part for instruction. Here is one way: When the pupils come into the assembly room, the leader first teaches them a new song, or explains a new order of service, or gives some other teaching that is needed. Any announcements which are necessary may also be given in this period. After 5 or 10 minutes, the leader sits down quietly, the candles (if any) are lighted, the doors are closed, and the prelude begins, followed by a brief service of worship, without further interruption. All of this can be done in 20 to 25 minutes if not too much teaching is attempted on any one day. If that much time is not available, it would be well to consider giving the whole assembly time on an occasional Sunday to instruction in worship.

A variation of this plan that can be used when the assembly room is available to a department for the entire church school period is to have an assembly at the opening of the session for a short period of training and announcements, then have the class sessions, and follow this with another assembly for worship only. Care must be taken to keep these assemblies brief, and to move classes to and from assemblies expeditiously, so as not to encroach on class time.

SUPERVISION OF WORSHIP

Though the general superintendent and other officers may not themselves conduct worship, they are nevertheless responsible for the training of worship leaders, and supervision of worship for its improvement. Here is a place where the pastor can be of greatest assistance, because of his own training in public worship and his concern for developing a worshiping congregation.

Following are some ways in which the superintendent, with the help of the pastor and other officers, may improve the worship aspect of the curriculum:

1. Help the committee on Christian education and all the workers to see the importance of worship.

2. Provide the best possible conditions for worship, by assignment of worship groups to the most suitable rooms, and insisting that the rooms be properly arranged, kept clean and orderly, and ready for use when the time for worship comes. See that pianos are in tune, proper hymnbooks and other equipment provided.

3. Arrange a schedule which gives a favorable place to worship, and if necessary, provides for more than one use of the rooms that are best suited for worship.

4. Train the leaders of worship. This training should include (1) the meaning of worship, and its place in the church school curriculum, (2) the art of planning services of worship, (3) the materials for use in worship and where resources may be found, (4) best ways in teaching pupils in the art of group worship.

5. Instruct leaders of worship not to exceed the time allotted, so as not to encroach on the time available to teachers. If on occasion more time is needed, as for a speaker or an audio-visual, teachers should be notified in advance.

Leaders of worship may be depended on to do a good deal of self-training, but they need to be encouraged in this, and helped to find the necessary guidance. Personal conferences with leaders, especially those who have been newly appointed, are a desirable means of meeting their immediate needs, in relation to the age of pupils whom they are leading. If such conferences are related to visits to the department for observation, they will be the more effective.

Sessions of the workers' conference may be devoted to the improvement of worship. Teachers as well as worship leaders can profit by such training.

Worship leaders may be encouraged to attend training schools and summer conferences where specialized training in worship may be had.

Most of what has been said applies to platform leadership of worship. Musical leadership is of equal importance. On this matter, Irwin G. Paulsen makes the following pertinent statement:

> The majority of accompanists are sufficiently skilled at least to play the notes; yet many are hopeless when it comes to playing accompaniments to hymns that literally inspire the right sort of singing. A practical suggestion is to "coach" the pianist and organist in the playing of hymns to the end that the tune shall be played "according to the words." The player should observe the phrases of each line and verse (commas *can* be put into the playing of a hymn), should suit the volume to the mood or content, and observe the natural climaxes, present in most tunes, and also the climactic verse which the hymn itself so often possesses.[4]

Here are ten questions that may be used by worship leaders for self-improvement, or by the superintendent in observing worship services:

1. Was the service well prepared in advance, with

---

[4] Paulsen, I. G., *The Church School and Worship,* p. 90. Macmillan, 1940.

proper spiritual preparation of leaders and pupils prior to the service?

2. Does the service have a central theme, and are the materials used so related to the theme as to provide unity?

3. Does the service center on the worship of God (not the entertainment of the pupils), and have something important to say about his relation to us and our relation to him?

4. Do the materials used give a Christian interpretation of God, and are they in the comprehension of the pupils? (Note especially the prayers of the leader.)

5. Do the hymns have literary and artistic merit, and are they suited for Christian worship?

6. Is the leader sincere and reverent, and does his leadership inspire the spirit of worship?

7. Is there reverent good order, with pupils attentive and responsive, participating in singing and responses, and seeming to achieve communion with God?

8. Are the ushering, offering, and other elements requiring pupil activity handled effectively and with reverence?

9. Is the room well arranged, clean, orderly, properly heated and ventilated?

10. Is opportunity provided in the session for training in worship? (This may not be true for every session, but the results of training should be evident.)

The book by I. G. Paulsen, previously cited, gives a more elaborate check list on pp. 95-96, on which a few of the above questions are based.

8 IMPROVING TEACHING

This chapter will deal with some of the problems in administration and supervision that are related to class teaching. It is the teachers who are primarily responsible for teaching the curriculum, and it is they who have the most intimate relations with the pupils and their parents. No matter how good the organization, or how excellent the curriculum materials, the program will not be effective unless the teachers make it so.

THE TEACHER'S TASK

Teachers need to be helped to see the importance of their particular place in the total program. There are certain conditions which must be met if teaching is to achieve its purpose.

1. *The Class.* A class is more than a collection of individuals of about the same age who are grouped together for convenience in teaching. It must be a *group* in the true sense of that word, in which members have a wholesome relationship with each other as well as with the teacher.

There needs to be friendliness, mutual respect, cooperation, purpose. Each person should sense his worth to the group, as well as the worth of each other member. Each member must accept the restrictions as well as the rights and privileges which belong to group living. At its best, a church school class is such a group that in it each member can be his own best self, under the inspiration of Christian ideals. It is the Christian fellowship of the church in miniature. To change a collection of individual boys and girls into such a group is one of the first tasks of the teacher.

A class is a group in fellowship with each other and the teacher, with a definite purpose. Its purpose is to learn discipleship. It is engaged on an exciting adventure for truth about God in his relation to man, and man's proper response in obedience and faith. The age of pupils will determine what form this quest will take, for the purpose must be one in which each pupil can share and not just something which is imposed by a teacher. On the other hand, the teacher must be accepted by the pupils as a mature friend who will guide them in developing purposes, carrying out interesting activities, and finding necessary information and other resources. The program of class work is not just the teacher's, not just the pupils', but a cooperative adventure in Christian learning and living.

Not all classes are like this. Perhaps few classes can achieve this ideal. But it is an ideal for which every teacher should strive if he wants his work to bear its best fruit.

2. *Knowing the Pupils.* To develop fruitful class work, a teacher must know each individual pupil. This begins with the simple matter of learning the names, and calling each by his proper name. Some teachers accomplish this on the first Sunday or two by having each pupil pin on himself a card on which his name has been printed in large

letters. Such a device also helps pupils to learn each other's names. Teachers should reciprocate by introducing themselves, and also wearing a name card or writing the name on the chalk board.

This is only a first step. Acquaintance must quickly go beyond names to information about each individual, and the development of friendly personal relations. For pupils who are able to write, some teachers find it helpful to have each fill out an information sheet.

Page 136 presents an example of a form for this purpose. It may be mimeographed on a sheet 8½ inches by 11 inches in size.

Knowing the pupil includes being acquainted with his home background. This is best achieved through home visits. If a visit is made to each home early in the year, it will establish a friendly rapport with parents which can be utilized throughout the year. Whatever else may be planned by way of church school and home relationships, the most fruitful contact will be that made by the teachers. The teacher should be primarily responsible for "follow-up" of pupils when they are persistently absent, or when a home contact needs to be made for other reasons.

Such personal acquaintance with individual pupils will accomplish three things: (1) It will help the teacher in developing a class program which captures the interests and utilizes the abilities of the class members. (2) It will help him to understand each individual pupil and go a long way toward solving discipline problems before they arise. (3) It will cause him to teach living persons instead of subject matter, and change an arduous task into a constant joy.

3. *The Class Program.* What has just been said does not imply that a teacher will follow the whims of pupils,

LET'S GET ACQUAINTED

My name is_____ My nickname is_____

I live at _____ My telephone number is _____

I go to _____ School. My grade is _____

I am _____ years old. My birthday is _____

My father's work is_____

My mother does_____ does not_____work away from home. I have _____

brothers and_____sisters. Other adults than parents in the home _____

The things I do best at school are:

1_____ 2._____

My hardest study at school is _____

The things I like best at Sunday school are:

1_____ 2._____

I belong to a choir_____ Scouts_____ Campfire Girls_____

Y.M.C.A. club_____

My favorite game is _____ My pet is a _____

My hobby is_____ I take_____lessons.
                                          special

The longest trip I ever took was to _____ My favorite book is_____

At home I help in these ways:

_____

If I could spend one day just as I please, I would do these things:

1._____ 2._____

The three things I want more than anything else are:

1._____ 2._____ 3._____

The three loveliest things I know are:

1._____ 2._____ 3._____

Three kinds of work I would like to do when I am grown are: 1._____
2._____ 3._____

Adapted from a paper prepared for Columbia University by Louise
Benckenstein Griffiths and Florence Martin.

wherever they may lead. Good teaching requires a purpose and program established by the church school and administered by the teacher, within which there is room for the development of pupils' interests and activities.

To start with, the teacher has the established curriculum of the church school. He must seek to understand and teach this as faithfully as possible. To do otherwise will lead to chaos so far as any definite plan for the church school is concerned. Within this curriculum, he may practice wide latitude in adapting his plans to the needs of class. Creative imagination is required to make a printed course come to life in a class.

For each class session, there needs to be a plan which is well thought out in advance, including purposes, what is to be done, materials to be used, assignments for the next session. Pupils may help make this session plan, but unless the teacher has a good idea in advance of what is appropriate procedure, he is in no position to give the pupils the guidance that they have a right to expect from him.

STANDARDS FOR TEACHERS

Most church school teachers are not professionally trained. They need help in developing a high conception of their work. Enthusiastic response to the call to teach and joy in the opportunity are indispensable to good teaching. When teachers have once caught this spirit, they need no persuasion to accept high standards.

It is helpful to make clear to teachers what is expected of them at the time when they are appointed. Minimum expectation should include at least the following:

1. *Regular Attendance.* Nothing short of an ideal of every-Sunday attendance is adequate. Classes will not develop good morale and interest if the teacher does not set

an example. The problem of maintaining continuity of interest and work with only one session each week is already a difficult one, and should not be further complicated by even occasional teacher absences. The suggestion is sometimes heard that two persons may share the work of a class, each taking responsibility on alternate Sundays or on alternate months. The plan of having two persons share in teaching a class is in itself a good one, provided both are present most of the time, and both share fully in planning for the class sessions. For them to alternate as teachers, with only one present at a session, is not good practice. Younger children need the sense of security that comes from having the same adults present with them each session, and older pupils need the support to faithful attendance and work that comes from knowing that the teacher will always be there.

To faithful attendance must be added the expectation of early arrival. Teachers cannot do their best work if they rush in at the last moment. Time should be allowed for checking on the classroom and materials to be used, and for greeting the pupils when they arrive. Some teachers utilize the pre-session period, the time after the first pupils arrive and before the formal opening, as a most fruitful opportunity for personal contact with individuals and allowing them to share in preparation for the class session. It reduces discipline problems if pupils are involved in useful activity as soon as they come in.

2. *Faithful Preparation.* Most of the failures in teaching can be traced to the twin faults of "too little and too late" by way of lesson preparation. What is required is both long-range planning and intensive week-by-week preparation. At the beginning of a new course, the teacher needs to make a general survey of the whole course, for

individual lessons do not stand in isolation from each other. There is a purpose for the whole course to which each individual session makes a contribution. This survey will not only give general orientation in the nature and content of the course, but will also indicate materials such as audio-visuals which should be ordered, activities which need to be planned long in advance, and background reading which the teacher needs to do for the course as a whole.

Preparation for each session should include intensive study of both teacher's and pupil's manuals, Bible passages included, and background information which the teacher needs to acquire. When this has been done, the teacher needs to make the lesson his own by thinking through what the purpose should be for his particular class, how this purpose may best be achieved through what the teacher will do in class and what the pupils will be asked to do, and what will be needed by way of resources, such as pictures, books, and working materials. Finally the plan for the session should be written out and mastered to the point where it can be freely used in the class session, with variations from it as the occasion may require. Such preparation cannot be made if it is left to the end of the week, but must be begun early. In fact, planning must begin more than a week in advance if pupil assignments are to be made.

Most teachers need training in proper methods of lesson preparation. Such training can best be given in workshop sessions in which the teachers of a department, under competent leadership, plan together for the lessons which will be taught on subsequent Sundays. Chapters 1 and 2 in *If Teaching Is Your Job* by J. L. Lobingier will be found useful in helping teachers with preparation as well as with conducting the class session.

3. *Participation in Training.* Most of the training that teachers receive must be acquired after they have assumed teaching responsibilities. This should not be deplored, because training can be made most effective when it is related to the actual experience of teaching. But it requires that teachers accept participation in training activities as a part of their responsibilities. Training opportunities will be discussed in a later chapter. Teachers should expect to attend workers' conferences of the whole school staff as well as departmental conferences, training classes and summer schools, and give some time to reading workers' magazines and books.

4. *Home Contacts.* Effective Christian teaching will rarely happen if the teacher does not have a friendly personal relation with each pupil. This comes in part through class activities, but must go beyond this to personal relations with the pupil and his parents. Hence any statement of standards for teachers should include responsibility for personal cultivation of each pupil. In most cases, the relation between pupil and church school teacher will be the closest tie that a child has with his church.

Some churches have found it helpful to develop a statement of standards for teachers, a copy of which is given to each teacher at the time of appointment. It is a good educational exercise for teachers to develop such standards cooperatively in the workers' conference. One of our correspondents, who is appropriately named Mrs. Eager, reports gratifying response from teachers to such a plan. Following are the standards they established:

(1) Regular attendance
(2) Thorough lesson preparation
(3) Each department head or his representative present 30 minutes before Sunday school begins

(4) Each teacher present 15 minutes before Sunday school begins; no teacher absent from opening worship except by permission

(5) Department head notified at least 3 days in advance of a necessary absence

(6) Each teacher and officer to keep accurate and detailed records of the pupils in his charge

(7) Regular attendance at monthly teachers' meeting

Not all workers agree that formalized standards are a good thing. There are some who fear that they may "scare off" prospective teachers, or simply be ignored. In such case, the standards which the officers would like to maintain will be passed on informally as general guidance to the workers in workers' conferences, and in personal conference at the time when the duties of a new teacher are explained to him.

HOME WORK

Should pupils be expected to do outside work for church school sessions? This question may be answered on four levels.

1. To be effective, Christian education must be related to all of life. What the pupil is, and is becoming, grows out of a multitude of relationships and activities in home, school, and community, as well as in church. In turn, the results of Christian teaching are measured by the extent to which it affects daily life through the new knowledge, attitudes, and skills which are being learned. At this level, "home work" is an integral part of every good curriculum.

2. A second level of out-of-school activity includes the use of materials which are to be taken home for informal use and enjoyment, but which nevertheless contribute to Christian education. This may include reading books, story

papers, devotional booklets, pictures, prayers, missionary materials, and suggestions for interesting things to do. If such materials are interesting to the pupil and their use is encouraged, this kind of home work presents no problem.

3. A third level of outside work is that which is related to pupil participation in church school class or department, for which preparation needs to be made. This may include preparation for taking part in a worship service, serving on a committee, being an officer in a youth group, bringing clippings and objects of interest related to class or department work, holding interviews and reporting on them, reporting on newspaper and magazine items of interest or on some unusual experience. Such outside work is a part of any program which achieves good pupil participation.

4. No one will question the value of outside work on the above three levels, and a good church school will experience little difficulty in getting it done. The real problem is at the fourth level. Should pupils be expected to do home study in preparation for church school sessions? This question does not apply to younger pupils, but becomes important for those who teach in junior and older departments.

There are some (especially parents) who object to making the church school like the day school. They argue that it should be more like the church service—an experience of worship and fellowship, with stories, discussion of religious problems, and so on—than like a school in the usual sense of the word. It is not to be doubted that much of the value of Christian education comes through the experience of fellowship and participation, under the auspices of the church.

But there is another side to the question. Christian education also requires the learning of a great deal of knowledge. Can this be done unless the practices of a good school are maintained? The ignorance of most church people concerning the Bible, the history of the church, and other elements of Christian knowledge is evidence that past policies with reference to home study have not been effective. In consideration of this problem, let us look at these facts:

(1) A vast amount of subject matter is included in church school curricula, which it is hopefully expected will be learned by the pupils.

(2) The nature of learning is such that it does not come about except through the pupil's effort, in applying his mind to the mastery of what is to be learned.

(3) The time available in the sessions of the church school—for many pupils not more than an hour each week —is too brief to accomplish what must be done, without additional outside work.

(4) The attitude of many pupils in church school classes is not conducive to effective learning.

Are we not forced to conclude that we will never succeed in teaching the content of the curriculum unless we can lay some claim on the pupil's effort outside the church school sessions? But how can we get pupils to accept and do their assignments? Most teachers will testify that this question has no easy answer. Yet if home work is necessary, we must by all means try to get it done.

In view of the voluntary nature of Christian education, the problem may never be fully solved in any class or church school. There is evidence, however, that church schools which have consistently worked at the problem have had a gratifying measure of success. Those who would make a persistent effort at a solution will find the following suggestions helpful:

(1) Develop a policy for the whole church school as a part of the training of workers.

(2) Use a curriculum series which provides adequate and attractive materials for the pupils. Bound textbooks are better than flimsy pamphlets.

(3) Make it a policy of the whole church school to expect respectable work from pupils. If all pupils are expected to accept home assignments from the age when they are first able to do so, there will be less resistance. If one or a few teachers only require what others do not, they will naturally meet with indifference or objection.

(4) Explain to parents why home work is necessary, and ask their cooperation in getting it done.

(5) Make definite and clear assignments, so that pupils will know exactly what is expected of them. Write these on the blackboard or give each a written memorandum. In the case of younger pupils, inform their parents of what has been assigned, by means of postcards or written memoranda taken home by the pupils.

(6) Until the habit of home work has been established, remind the pupils toward the end of the week. With a whole week between sessions, it is so easy for them to forget. If the reminder is by postcard or telephone call, parents are likely to see it or hear about it.

(7) Have work sessions with classes or committees, in addition to class sessions.

(8) Integrate assignments with class work as closely as possible, so that home work will be meaningful. Hold pupils to account for what they have been asked to do, through calling on them to contribute in class discussion, or through individual reports.

(9) Give some kind of recognition for work done, such as displaying a class chart showing assignments made and the names of those who have completed them, or including home work done as an item on reports made to the home.

9 AWARDS AND DISCIPLINE

There are two problems that arise so frequently in discussions of church school administration that they deserve extended treatment. One is the question of whether some kind of recognition in the form of awards, prizes, and gifts should be given pupils because of work well done and to stimulate better performance. The other concerns discipline, and how good order may be maintained.

AWARDS AND OTHER RECOGNITION

Should awards, prizes, and other recognition be given for special achievement? If so, what kinds and under what conditions? The church school has been an open field for contests, attendance pins, and other forms of artificial stimulation. It cannot be doubted that these at times lead to temporary spurts of interest and effort, but do they ever have permanent value? May they even do actual harm?

1. *Basic Considerations.* Questions such as these can be answered only in relation to basic considerations which

concern the nature and purpose of what we are trying to accomplish in the church school.

(1) Christian fellowship, with mutual respect and love, is a necessary condition for Christian education. Any scheme which makes for rivalries, which requires some to fail that others may win, which generates selfish pride in the fortunate ones, is to be avoided because it destroys fellowship.

(2) A Christian should attend his church because it satisfies his soul's craving for God and Christian nurture, not for some worldly reward. This is a truth which should be learned from earliest childhood, and it is folly to teach otherwise by offering external rewards for what should be its own best reward. Rewards have a tendency to make people turn inward and think about themselves rather than the value of what they are doing.

(3) When the program is of high quality, pupils will be interested and do not need artificial inducements to attend and participate. On the other hand, no such devices will serve to bolster up and compensate for a poor program.

(4) If recognition is to be given, it should be based on achievements which are important in Christian growth, not merely on such externals as attendance. It is of course desirable that pupils attend regularly, but what they learn depends more on the motive for attendance than mere physical presence. Unfortunately, it is difficult to check up on the things which are most important, and the effort to measure and recognize them may actually be harmful to their achievement.

(5) Before adopting any plan for awards, consideration must be given to all the possible results, the bad as well as the good. Can it be administered with justice? Even so simple a matter as awards for attendance raises vexing

questions of what constitutes excusable absence, and whether errors were made in recording attendance. Will it have bad effects? Granted that a contest or a plan for awards will get certain results, are they all good? After its initial impact, will it motivate only the few who would be faithful anyway, while those who most need encouragement fall by the wayside? Will the desire to keep up their records cause pupils to attend when they are ill and thus spread colds and other diseases? In case of a contest, will it breed ill-will, and perhaps cause a reaction after the contest is over which leaves the situation worse than it was before? Is it too expensive? Badges and pins and other rewards can run into big money.

(6) On the positive side, let us grant that it is a trait of human nature to respond favorably to some recognition for achievement. When standards are clearly defined and accepted by the pupils as being fair and necessary, most of them will respond favorably. Satisfactory achievement may properly be recognized so as to give the pupil a sense of work well done and encouragement to future effort, but the emphasis should always be on the value of what has been accomplished, not on material awards.

2. *Guiding Principles.* Certain principles in awarding recognition follow from the above considerations.

(1) An interesting and effective program is the only adequate basis for getting pupil attendance and effort. Hence, any plan for recognition should be based on satisfactory progress in the main purposes of the church school.

(2) The motive for achievement should be based on the intrinsic values that come from work well done, not on some material reward or honor which generates false motives.

(3) Recognition should be equally possible for all

pupils, and not favor those with special talents and superior native ability. Pupils should be challenged to improve their own records rather than being put in competition with others.

(4) Standards on which recognition is based should cover many aspects of performance, such as class and department participation, attitudes and conduct, knowledge acquired, home work, memory work, as well as attendance.

(5) Workers should constantly bear in mind that the primary aim is growth in discipleship, and that performance according to objective standards is only a symptom of and never to be fully equated with inner growth.

While the school as a whole may set certain standards of work, there is wide variation in what may be expected of pupils of different ages. Each department will need its own specific standards and plans for recognition. The final unit of administration will be the class. Any teacher may establish his own set of standards, in harmony with any plans for the department and school, and if this is done in cooperation with the pupils so that such requirements become their own, so much the better. Check-up will usually be made in class. Most of this may come as a part of normal class procedure, as the pupil uses in class discussion what he has learned. Written examinations and other forms of testing are appropriate for older classes. The record of each pupil's accomplishment may be displayed in the form of a simple chart. The emphasis should always be on satisfaction in work well done, not on the teacher's approval or the pupil's pride in doing better than others.

3. *Report Cards.* Some church schools issue regular reports to the home, and in some cases individual teachers do this even when it is not a plan of the school. This is a good plan, provided that the report covers not simply at-

tendance but other items of significance in the pupil's progress, that the teachers keep a running record of the pupils' work as a basis for the report, and that there is opportunity for conference with parents, when desirable, as a result of the report.

4. *Giving Bibles.* Some churches give a Bible to pupils as a prize for some unusual achievement. Our reverence for the Bible should not lead us to approve this any more than other material gifts. There is, however, another kind of presentation which has no relation to awards. This is the plan of having the church present a Bible to every pupil when he reaches the age where he can read it and use it in his church school work. An appropriate time for this is when the pupil is promoted from the primary to the junior department. If promotions are made in the spring, it may be better to wait and make the presentation when these pupils enrol in the fall, so that use of the Bible may follow immediately, under the guidance of the teacher.

In support of this plan, let it be said that it is a suitable recognition of the pupil's completion of a stage of his work and entry upon a period when a new type of work is expected of him, it provides each pupil with his own Bible, and it assures that all pupils have the same version.

Since the Revised Standard Version of the Bible is generally used in church school literature, this is the version that should be presented. The edition presented should be of good quality, in type size which the pupil can easily read, and attractively and durably bound. If this requires an expenditure which the church cannot well afford, parents may be asked to share the cost. This has the further value of emphasizing that Christian education is a joint responsibility of home and church. Since some pupils enter the church school after the age when Bibles are given, it is wise for the church to have a supply which may be sold to such pupils at cost.

5. *Gifts.* Should teachers be expected to give birthday and Christmas gifts to their pupils? Certainly they should not be *expected* to do this. But if some teachers give gifts, others may be forced to do likewise to avoid unfavorable comparisons. For this reason some church school staffs have wisely made a rule that no teacher is to give gifts other than simple greeting cards. There are other ways of showing appreciation and affection than by material gifts.

It was once a fairly general practice for church schools to give candy and other presents to pupils at Christmas. Happily this emphasis on receiving has been superseded by an emphasis on giving through White Gifts or some other suitable service project. It would seem that the practice of giving Christmas presents to pupils can be justified only in cases where they are so impoverished that the church can be of help in bringing this small measure of pleasure into their lives.

DISCIPLINE

A parent was asked why his child was no longer attending Sunday school and he replied, "We do not want him to learn the kind of misbehavior to which he is exposed there." A teacher stated as the reason for her resignation: "I like to teach but I am tired of the constant battle to get good order. I have to spend so much time on discipline, there is no chance to do constructive teaching." A boy gave as his reason for preferring the church service to the church school, "There is too much chaos in Sunday school." Another boy said he dropped out of Sunday school because "we never do anything worthwhile, just cut up." Cases like this could be multiplied.

Forty years ago a great Christian educator wrote:

Courtesy, accuracy, promptness, regularity, industry, responsibility, obedience, reverence, are among the virtues which
enter into the fiber of our moral life. A school which toler-
ates discourtesy without rebuke; which permits irregularity
of attendance and tardiness without penalty; which accepts
inaccurate or poorly prepared work, makes assignments and
permits pupils to come unprepared without reproof; which
condones the most patent exhibitions of disobedience and
irreverence without corresponding exhibition of the wrath
of an outraged law, cannot expect to be rated in the community as a moral institution. Such an institution under-
mines the moral life of the nation. And yet this is the picture of multitudes of church schools.[1]

Church schools have not changed much in our generation! If Athearn's argument is sound, who of us can escape
its condemnation? Probably a majority of church school
workers will agree that their greatest problem is discipline.
But just what do we mean by discipline, and what constitutes good order? The following interpretation will vary
somewhat from that implied in the above quotation, but
will agree completely with its insistence on the need for
good order in the church school.

1. *What is discipline?* Good order exists in a church
school when pupils and teachers are directing their ener-
gies to the accomplishment of the purposes of the school,
with a minimum of confusion, distraction, and irrelevant
activity. Good order requires discipline. The disciplined
person is free to achieve worthy purposes for himself and
his group because he is able to direct his energy into right
channels, and restrain himself from pursuing irrelevant or

---

[1] Athearn, W. S., *The Organization and Administration of the Church
School*, pp. 322, 323. Pilgrim Press, 1917.

unworthy ends. He "plays by the rules" of group living and work because he knows that rules and regulations are necessary for the success of any social group. He accepts the need for authority as well as the need for participation on his part. Learning self discipline is a necessary part of growing to maturity.

The teacher's concern with discipline is positive as well as negative. On the positive side, it is a matter of helping the pupil to understand what is right behavior, find worthy goals to which to direct his energy, gain self control, take pride in good workmanship and conduct appropriate to his age. On the negative side it consists of preventing undesirable conduct.

It is necessary for a church school to maintain good order for two important reasons: (1) as an end in itself: teaching self discipline is an essential element in teaching for Christian living; (2) as a means to an end: an organized program of work cannot be carried on without it.

2. *What is good discipline?* Considered from the point of view of the teacher's approach to securing and maintaining good order, we may distinguish three types of discipline:

(1) *Authoritarian Control.* This is implied in the quotation on page 152. It assumes that leaders are in control and pupils are to obey their instructions and commands. Pupils are told what to do. They are given rules and standards made by the leader. They are marched in ordered lines from class to department. They are required to raise their hands for the privilege of speaking. They are admonished to be quiet. They are threatened with unhappy consequences for misconduct.

(2) *Cooperative Participation.* This assumes that pupils can learn to become a creative social group. Pupils help

make their own rules. They share in choosing purposes and activities. They are free to speak to each other and to the leader as their work may require. Their opinions are respected. They are allowed to be active and even noisy, as long as their activity and noise are the expression and result of useful work. The need for right conduct is interpreted by the leader and enforced when necessary, but not by methods which destroy the relationship of respect and love. Standards of good work are set by the leader in cooperation with the pupils, and maintained through pride in high quality rather than by rewards or threats. Leaders who practice this type of discipline have a conviction that self discipline rather than external control is the ultimate objective.

(3) *Laissez Faire.* Some leaders believe that when pupils are allowed to do as they please, they will love the teacher and the church school more. Hence, they shun hard requirements and strict standards. They are, of course, not in favor of chaos, but hope that the respect for the leader and the appeal of the work will be sufficient for reasonably good conduct without invoking the pressure of authority. They are inclined to take the attitude that "Children are like that, and you can't expect too much of them."

The first and third positions have been stated in extreme form for contrast. It is to be said for the first that leaders of the church school are responsible for what goes on there and should not shirk their authority. Education always requires effort, and will not often result from the pupil's own native interest without some support from authority. The third position is based on the false assumption that pupils will like church school when it is made easy for them. There is abundant evidence that pupils are more interested when they are challenged with worthwhile requirements than when they are allowed just to have a good time in accordance with their own wishes. If we should have to choose between the first and the third, we would prefer the first. Fortunately the middle position can capture what is good in both of the others. We would support this type of discipline for Christian education for the following reasons:

(1) It respects the pupil as a person and utilizes his capacities for self-direction at whatever stage of maturity he has reached. It is aimed as much at the pupil's own self development in mature conduct as at achieving external quiet and order so that class work may go on.

(2) It enhances the development of Christian community in every group, with love and respect of the members for each other and for their leader.

(3) Learning is more effective when the pupil shares in setting goals and is otherwise an active participant in the process.

(4) It gives educational value to the relationships in the church school as well as to the studies which are pursued.

(5) It provides for a relationship between pupils and leaders through which the character and faith of the latter can make its best impact.

It must be evident that discipline does not apply to pupils only, but to teachers as well. Prompt and regular attendance, adequate preparation, effort to understand the pupils, visiting the homes, maintaining a loving relationship with each pupil, justice, patience, and prayer are some of the elements which enter into the discipline of the teacher. The problem of discipline may center more in teachers than in pupils!

We have emphasized the positive aspects of discipline. Good order is one of the lessons in character which the church school should teach. It results from an orderly program, high standards, respect for pupils and their interests, utilization of the natural impulses to activity, and sharing in democratic procedure. This kind of discipline is present in every good curriculum. It is most effective when it is such a natural part of the life of the church school that there are few evidences of effort to maintain it.

Unfortunately, it is the experience of most workers that even though they may strive for this positive kind of discipline, pupils will not always respond. There are instances of misbehavior and lack of cooperation which require direct attention if work is to go on. To use an analogy, good health is the normal condition of the human body, but the body is also subject to ills and diseases which must be treated if the healthy condition is to be restored. Many church schools are very sick indeed.

3. *Why do pupils misbehave?* There is always a reason for conduct. When pupils misbehave, it is because they get more satisfaction from wrong conduct than from right. A child is full of energy, curiosity, and a desire for recognition. When the regular activity of the church school does not provide a desirable outlet, he will find other ways for expression. What is considered bad conduct may be bad only by the standards of the teacher, not by the standards of the pupil. It is more natural for a child to do what the adult world expects of him than to set himself against it, but he is also very sensitive to the standards of his own group.

In order to have a tolerable condition in which work can go on, a teacher must often deal with instances of misbehavior directly, as a doctor may prescribe aspirin to relieve pain. But the doctor seeks for the causes of pain in order to correct them. So the teacher must get at the causes of misbehavior and correct them if healthy good order is to become a natural condition of his group. What are some of the underlying causes for poor discipline?

(1) In some church schools it is just the fashion to be noisy, disorderly, and irresponsible. It is unfortunate that the institution which seeks to teach virtue has been allowed to become a place where the elements which enter into the very fibre of moral character are violated, but such is often the case. Pupils misbehave simply because everybody else is doing it.

(2) What is considered misbehavior may be nothing more than the natural energy of the pupil expressing itself in wrong channels, because no right channels have been provided for it. If the pupil is bored with his class session or department service, he is likely to find some way to create a little excitement.

(3) Pupils may engage in acts of misbehavior because they have never been taught what is the right behavior, in either the home or the church school. Discipline must be taught, and it requires just as much patience and effort to teach right conduct as it does to teach the content material of the curriculum.

(4) Causes of misbehavior are sometimes to be traced to the curriculum. If the church school material is poorly graded, too advanced or too juvenile for the pupils' maturity, deals with subjects in which they have no interest, it is hard to keep their thought and activity centered on the work of the church school.

(5) While teachers are too ready to blame the home for all their troubles, it is nevertheless true that at times the causes for poor discipline can be traced to the home. The pupil acts as he is allowed to act at home. Or it may be that home discipline is so strict and arbitrary that he re-

acts against it when he has the opportunity to do so. There may be other home conditions which have a bearing on conduct in the church school.

(6) Poor discipline may result from the fact that pupils have not accepted what is done in the church school as being of any importance to them. Many teachers are in the predicament of a salesman who is peddling a product that nobody wants. On the other hand, pupils are likely to give their interest and attention to what they consider worthwhile, and to the achievement of goals which they have accepted.

(7) Probably more than anything else, poor teaching is the cause of problems in discipline. When teachers are unwilling themselves to undergo the discipline necessary to prepare for a teaching session which can be exciting to the pupils and keep them at work every minute, they can hardly expect the pupils to give their wholehearted attention.

(8) Poor discipline may be the result of the conditions under which the church school works. If the class or department room is over-crowded, poorly ventilated, unattractively furnished, inadequately cleaned, not properly equipped with chairs and tables, and worse still, if the teacher makes no effort to arrange the room as attractively and advantageously as possible, this invites restlessness and poor conduct. Where more than one class has to meet in the same room, there is an initial problem of maintaining good order, which may be aggravated by poor arrangement of classes, teachers talking too loudly, and officers performing their work too conspicuously.

(9) Poor administrative procedure may be the cause of many discipline problems. This concerns such matters as the taking of records, distribution of supplies, movement

of pupils to departments and classes, and inadequate adherence to proper schedules.

(10) Some pupils may be problem cases because they have unfulfilled needs, such as the need for understanding and love, security, recognition, and self-appreciation, which they are trying to satisfy. Misbehavior resulting from such causes must still be dealt with, but it is much easier to handle when the causes are recognized.

(11) Are there some pupils who are just natural troublemakers, who delight in misbehavior rather than in good conduct? It is our contention that it is more natural for children to work with the group and with the leader than against them. Evidences to the contrary, of which there may be many, should be recognized as symptoms of other causes at work rather than a sign of depravity.

4. *How to Maintain Good Order.* To understand the need for discipline and the causes of bad order is not enough. We are usually faced with an actual situation which must be met. How do we get and maintain good order?

Let's get one point clear. When the officers and teachers work for good order, they are not setting themselves against the pupils. They are working with the pupils to achieve something which is in the pupils' own best interest, and usually something the pupils themselves want.

The causes of poor behavior in the church school which have been listed indicate that it rarely results from perverseness or "badness." The pupils' attitudes and conduct which are so annoying are usually but symptoms of something wrong which lies much deeper. It indicates failure of officers and teachers rather than of pupils. These causes must be eliminated if the cure is to be effected. Here are some suggestions of what may be done by the officers and staff of a church school which wants to make a concerted attack on the problem.

(1) Study the problem in your church school. Get away from mere complaint and criticism of pupils or their parents and look at the facts. What are the causes of poor discipline in your situation? A constructive program might include some of the following elements:

(2) If a fashion of poor discipline has developed, decide what would be a reasonable expectation of good order and enlist all the workers in striving for it. Do not leave individual teachers to struggle with achieving that which the spirit of the school is against. Make it an educational venture by sharing your ideals with the pupils and encouraging them to accept the new order. Remember that education is slow, that teaching of right conduct must be done over and over. Discipline is a part of good teaching. Don't expect miracles. Ponder these words:

> All teaching is slow; teaching anything is, but you keep at it. You talk. When the behavior happens again, you discuss again. You plan with your students again. You are right on the job. You are prepared to talk and discuss and analyze and evaluate a hundred times, if need be. . . . In academic areas, if a youngster does not learn the first time, you are not dismayed. You are not even discouraged. You try and try again. You try to discover each child's particular private stumbling block. You look for different examples that will make the point clear. You keep your eyes open for small signs of progress. You know that someone else, following you, will build on the foundation you lay. In teaching discipline you will have many invitations to reach for a club to pound the lesson home in a jiffy. Remember: you do not use a club in the rest of your teaching. You accept that learning comes slowly, that it takes a long time.[2]

---

[2] Hymes, James L., Jr., *Behavior and Misbehavior*. Prentice-Hall, 1955.

(3) If administrative procedures have been a cause of trouble, try to correct these where they are at fault. Adopt a better plan for enrolling pupils, taking records, distributing materials. Start on time, and make sure that teachers and department leaders are ready to begin at the appointed time. Have workers come early so as to channel the activity of early pupils before they get out of hand. Adopt orderly procedures for movement of classes during the session, eliminate interruptions of classes for collecting records, distributing papers, making announcements, and so on.

(4) Consider whether the curriculum in classes and departments is such that pupils can honestly be expected to get excited about it. There is no solution to problems of discipline without the positive appeal of a good program. If lesson material is at fault, consider making a change. More likely what is needed is better use of material, with supplemental resources.

(5) Help teachers to see that most discipline problems arise out of their own inadequate preparation or lack of ingenuity in making sessions interesting. If lessons are so planned that the teacher can be free to teach pupils and not be tied to a book, take care of their individual needs, utilize their natural tendency to be active, most discipline problems are met before they arise. If something interesting is going on every minute, there is little opportunity for disorder. If the details of class management are properly handled, such as the seating of pupils, the distribution of materials, the taking of the record, many opportunities for disorder will be eliminated.

(6) Problems arising from poor housing and equipment may require capital expenditures for their solution. But with the exercise of ingenuity and imagination, much can

be done with existing resources. Rooms can be kept clean and in order. Class space can be rearranged for more effective use. Classes or departments can be shifted to make better use of available rooms. If the adult classes are occupying rooms which are more needed for the teaching of children, perhaps they can be persuaded to give up their rooms. Classes meeting in one large room can be re-arranged for greater separation, and sometimes protected from disturbing one another by the use of curtains or screens. If there is too much crowding, schedules can be devised which permit of more than one use of available space on a given Sunday. New equipment and supplies such as blackboards, storage cabinets, worship centers, maps, hymnbooks, and audio-visuals can be added without undue expense.

(7) Take parents into partnership with you in your attempt to establish good order. It usually does no good to heap complaint or blame on them. It is not likely that discipline problems will yield to long-range treatment from the home, though such problems may be discussed with parents if it is done with a view to trying to understand the pupil better. But parents can lend strong moral support to the church school if they show interest in it, interpret its objectives to their children, and give their backing to high standards of work and conduct. After all, the pupils are the children of these parents, and therefore the parents should be more concerned with what is happening in the church school than anyone else.

5. *Dealing with Individual Cases.* These are general approaches which may be made, and without such basic treatment the problems of discipline will not be solved. Even so, there will still be specific cases with which the teacher must deal. The following suggestions are offered

to teachers by way of dealing with individual pupils who constitute problems:

(1) Do not hesitate to insist on good order. You are responsible for maintaining the moral order of the church school, and cannot condone conduct which is out of keeping with its purposes. You have an obligation to those pupils who want to do serious work as well as to those who need your correcting influence.

(2) Your attitude should not be one of meting out blame or punishment, but of helping pupils to achieve right adjustment. The way to get rid of a problem child is to help him change so that he will no longer be a problem.

(3) Try to understand the individual pupil and discover the causes for his conduct. Friendship with the pupil and consultation with parents, public school teachers, and others who know him best will help you in gaining this understanding.

(4) Consider the age of the pupil. Make allowance for the impulsiveness, exuberance, and love of fun which are the marks of childhood. Do not expect him to act like a miniature adult.

(5) Make sure that the pupil understands what is expected of him. This applies to assignments and class work as well as to conduct in class and department.

(6) Enlist the pupil on your side by giving him opportunities to help you. Giving the trouble maker a job will not always solve discipline problems, but it does help when he feels that he has important things to do. Conduct class and other group sessions in such a way that the contributions of pupils are utilized, so that they may feel it to be their own session. If pupils come early, find ways to let them help prepare for the session, and thus divert them from the mischief they might otherwise get into.

(7) If the pupil's difficulty seems to be that he is shy, lacks security, needs love and appreciation, or craves recognition, handle your class session in such a way as to help meet his need. It is a mistake to let the brightest pupils give all the answers. Give the slower pupils something to do in which they also can excel.

(8) Never show irritation, or use harsh words, ridicule, or sarcasm. Treat the pupil as a person who deserves your respect. Do not raise your voice to out-shout class noise, but keep it at a natural level.

(9) Never indulge in vague threats which you have no way of carrying out. If something must be done to correct the pupil, do it promptly, with justice, and in such a way that the fellowship between you and the pupil is not broken.

(10) In case problems arise because a class or group is too large, an assistant can be useful in helping with details and in giving individual attention to pupils.

(11) If a serious situation requires the help of the superintendent or some other official, his function should not be that of a policeman, but that of a friend who works with the teacher in helping him master the situation.

(12) Should punishment ever be resorted to? Flagrant violation of rules and standards should have unpleasant consequences. But the question is, What kind of punishment? Treatment should be educative in correcting the evil, rather than a penalty for wrong committed. The only kind of punishment which is effective is that which follows misdeeds as a natural consequence. If isolation follows anti-social conduct, the culprit has only himself to blame. It must be admitted that punishment is hard to make effective. Unless the group is *with* the leader, the very act of administering penalties may lead to a kind of recognition

164

which does more harm than good. Hence, it is always better to work on the positive teaching side than to depend on penalties to get the desired results.

One wishes that a treatment of discipline could be so written that everyone who reads it would find a solution to all his problems. Unfortunately, this is not possible. No simple rules can be given which apply to all cases. The nature of each case depends on both the teacher and the pupils involved. We are convinced that sustained efforts will yield results.

For a fuller treatment of the problem of discipline, workers are advised to read chapter 9, "What About Discipline?", in *If Teaching Is Your Job* by John L. Lobingier, and *Behavior and Misbehavior* by James L. Hymes, Jr.

10 CHURCH SCHOOL AND HOME

Before there were Sunday schools, the home was expected to take full responsibility for the religious nurture of children. We are reminded of the words in Deuteronomy 6:6, 7: "And these words which I command you this day shall be upon your heart; and you shall teach them diligently to your children," and of how the faith of the young man Timothy, which Paul commends, "dwelt first in your grandmother Lois and your mother Eunice" (2 Tim. 1:5). Christian nurture is still primarily the responsibility of the home, and it is tragic when parents get the idea that they can discharge their duty by merely taking their children to Sunday school.

This statement is not intended to minimize the place of the church in Christian education. It is to recognize that at best the church school can but share with the home in a process to which each makes a contribution. Only the home can supply the warm Christian environ-

166

ment, the experience of love, the daily guidance in thought and conduct, which are so important in Christian nurture. The church on its part can continue and broaden this experience of Christian fellowship, and add systematic teaching of religion.

This recognition of the home as the primary instrument in Christian nurture does not make it a rival of the church or establish another "body of Christ" apart from the church. The Christian home is the church in action, for it is from the church that it receives its inspiration and guidance. This is inherent in Christian marriage. The church which is concerned for Christian nurture must be concerned with establishing and maintaining Christian homes.

The home is so important in religious life and development that one of the main concerns of the church needs to be with the establishment and maintenance of Christian families. It is beyond the scope of this book to treat this subject fully. To do so would require a separate volume, some of the chapters of which would be (1) the meaning of Christian marriage, (2) education of young people for Christian marriage and family life, (3) counseling with couples about to be married, (4) the significance of baptism or dedication of children, (5) helping young couples to make their home life Christian, (6) the Christian nurture of children in the home, (7) helps for parents in their work of Christian nurture, (8) how to deal with children's religious questions, (9) the family's relation to the church.

Since this book is addressed primarily to those concerned with the administration of the church school, we must limit our discussion to the interrelations which should be maintained between church school and home in the interest of making the church's program of Christian education most effective.

A POINT OF VIEW

The success of any plans for church school and home cooperation will depend on establishing the right point of view.

1. Many parents do not realize the importance of their part in Christian education. They regard the church school as an agency to serve them and their children without reciprocal obligations on them. Some even think that they are doing the church school a favor by sending their children!

On the contrary, parents should realize that it is they who are accountable to God for the Christian nurture of their children. When they brought their children for baptism or dedication, they answered "I do!" to the question "Do you promise in dependence on the grace of God, to bring up your child in the nurture and admonition of the Lord?" The church school can help parents in discharging this obligation, but it should not be asked to do it all. Parents should expect to share in the work of the church school and seek ways in which they can enhance its effectiveness, rather than grudgingly yielding to the requests which teachers make of them. If they take no part in the work of the church school, and perhaps even have no active relation to the church, there can be little hope that the effort of the church school alone will work in their children what they themselves are denying by example.

There are many parents who will gladly give their whole-hearted cooperation if what they are expected to do is made clear to them. Also, there are some who will send their children with no intention on their part to do anything beyond this. In the latter case, the church school teachers must recognize that they have a missionary opportunity and do the best they can to make up for the parents' neglect. Moreover, such parents may often be brought more fully into the church through their interest in their children.

2. Teachers need to realize that the task they undertake is one which can be achieved only by joint effort with the parents. They cannot do it alone, without support and cooperation from the home. Most teachers are aware of this, but do little or nothing about it because they assume (not without justice) that parents should show their interest without being prodded into it. Yet many parents do not know how to take hold on the problem, and some hesitate to take the initiative for fear of being thought meddlesome. Teachers should open the way through home visits and other contacts to make it easy and natural for parents to cooperate. In this respect teachers are like ministers, and every minister knows that if he would reach people effectively, he must take the initiative in going out to them.

It follows from our conception of the church as a Christian fellowship, worshiping and serving God and seeking to increase and extend its spirit, that every member should be concerned with making its teaching program effective. Parents above all others should respond to this obligation in view of their special responsibility to their own children. Hence teachers need not feel that they are asking a favor when they seek parental cooperation. In devising a plan for Christian education which depends on both the church and the home, the workers in the church school are providing a practical means for parents to discharge an obligation to their children and their church which in any case rests on them.

WHAT IS EXPECTED?

One of the first steps in establishing church school and home relationships is for both teachers and parents to be clear on what each expects of the other. Complaints about non-cooperation and vague admonitions to cooperate will do little good.

In numbers of parent-teacher conferences, the writer has had parents and teachers list and discuss what they feel they have a right to expect. The results of these discussions may be summarized as follows:

1. *What Parents Expect of Church School Teachers*

(1) Have a friendly interest in each pupil. Respect him as a person. Know his interests and his particular abilities and use them to draw him into class participation.

(2) Assume that parents are vitally interested in the religious development of their children. Help them to understand what you are trying to accomplish and to become familiar with the materials of the curriculum, and give them an opportunity to make suggestions. Share with them any evidence of interest and growth on the part of the child, and consult them on problems.

(3) Provide an interesting and worthwhile class program, so that the pupils can respect the church school and be challenged by it.

(4) Be present regularly, with a well-prepared lesson, so that pupils may sense your own appreciation of the importance of the church school. It is devastating to morale if pupils are frequently left with a substitute, or worse still, combined with another class.

(5) Establish and maintain high standards of discipline

and class work; remember that most pupils much prefer an orderly, purposeful session to one in which chaos and purposelessness prevail.

(6) When you assign home activities or make other requests, make these requirements quite definite, and in case of younger children let the parents know if they can help in getting them done. A typed slip of paper to take home, a postcard reminder, or a telephone call will be very helpful.

(7) Meet parents at least half way in making their personal acquaintance and in keeping contact.

2. *What Teachers Expect of Parents*

(1) See that the pupil is regularly present, on time, unless prevented by illness or other reason which would be accepted as legitimate by the public school.

(2) Encourage your child in his church school work by showing your interest in what he is doing, and participating yourself in the church school and church.

(3) Make it easy for the teacher to maintain mutually helpful contacts with you, by welcoming visits and telephone calls, and at times taking the initiative in sharing with the teacher any evidences of success or lack of success in what he is doing in the church school.

(4) Cooperate with the teacher in encouraging the pupil to do his assigned work, and bringing his church school materials each Sunday.

(5) Make a faithful effort to use the curriculum material provided for the home, such as parents' magazines, family books, adult study materials.

(6) Attend meetings of parents, parents' classes, and other events which may be held for the improvement of the church school, and for the guidance of families in Christian nurture. Is it too much to expect that such oc-

casions should be given priority over club meetings, social engagements, or a favorite TV program?

(7) Strive for a Christian family life which will support the church and its teaching.

Every teacher who has tried to get home cooperation knows, of course, that many parents are not interested in participating in the work of the church school to the extent indicated by these lists of desirable mutual relationships. However, many will become more interested when the effort is made to interpret to them how the home and church school must be related if Christian education is to be effective.

Teachers should not be expected to carry the entire burden of maintaining home cooperation. The policy of the whole church school should be one which relies on all teachers to make such efforts, and to support them in what they are expected to do.

PATHWAYS TO ACHIEVEMENT

Since effective Christian education can result only from a joint effort of church and home, ways must be found of bringing them into partnership. Any church school can improve its home relationships, but not without careful planning and consistent effort. Following are some plans which have been successfully used:

1. *Interpret Christian education to include the home.* Let it be understood that the sessions of the church school are but one part of the total program, to be matched by other parts which only the home can provide. Carry this conception into the planning of a curriculum that includes responsibilities which the home must assume.

This has not been the traditional conception of a church school, and must be interpreted to the whole church, as well as to individual families, if it is to be understood and accepted. One of the best opportunities for making such interpretation is at the time when new pupils are enrolled. This is an occasion of sufficient importance to justify a conference with the parents. In this conference, appreciation can be expressed for their confidence in this particular church school, while at the same time it is made clear that in enrolling the pupil, the church is expecting the parents to accept certain responsibilities. Most parents will be quick to understand that the church school with its limited time and other handicaps cannot accomplish what the parents expect of it, without their help. This conference provides an opportunity for explaining the curriculum and acquainting the parents with the lesson materials in use. It should result in a clear statement of just what parents can do, and open the way for continuing cooperation between teachers and parents. Such a conference, either at the church or in the home, should follow as soon as possible the enrollment of a new pupil.

For families already related to the church, the nursery roll or cradle roll provides an opportunity for establishing a relationship between the home and the church in Christian nurture, and may serve as a bridge for effecting the transition of the young child into the church school.

2. *Use curriculum material which provides for home activities.* Good curriculum materials recognize the place of the home in Christian education, and include materials for home use. The matter of home relationships is handled in one of several ways. In one series, quarterly magazines are provided in each department which enable parents to follow the week-by-week church school lessons. Another series provides quarterly books for the home which are not so directly related to the church school lessons, but

intended to provide plans and resources for religious activities in the home. Still another series provides family
books for use in parent study groups in the church. Several denominations have magazines which are aimed specifically at the development of Christian home life.

Providing parents with such materials is not in itself
effective in most cases. The materials must be interpreted
with respect to their purpose and value, and encouragement and guidance given to parents in their use. Nor can
guidance for home cooperation be given wholly through
printed material. Much will depend on specific plans made
by teachers through which parents can do their part in
making curriculum most effective.

If a change is made to a new type of curriculum material, several months may well be taken to acquaint the
church, and particularly the parents, with the reasons for
the change and the nature and merits of the new material
adopted. This is especially important if the new material
requires larger expenditures and more effort on the part
of the home.

3. *Have teachers visit in homes.* A single conference
with parents at the time a new pupil is enrolled is not
sufficient. Teachers in the church school should be in continuing relationship with the homes represented in their
classes. The best time to establish contact is through home
visits at the beginning of the church school year. Once this
personal acquaintance has been made and a relationship
established, it is not difficult to maintain it through telephone calls, letters, and casual contacts before and after
church service and at other church functions.

What should be the purpose of such visits? They will
accomplish at least the following: establish face to face
acquaintance between teacher and parents, with oppor-

tunity to share mutual interests; give opportunity to interpret the curriculum and class program, with specific suggestions of how parents can help; result in better acquaintance with the home life, activities, hobbies of the pupils; provide for exchange of information on evidence of the effectiveness of the church school; help establish rapport with the pupils.

Will parents welcome such visits? Most of them do. Take the case of Jimmie, who was something of a problem throughout the church school, and whose parents were not active in the church. One of Jimmie's teachers believed in home visits, and called on Jimmie's parents a number of times. Some years later Jimmie's mother remarked about this teacher to a friend: "So far as we are concerned, the only teacher Jimmie ever had in church school was Mr. —————. We did not even know the names of the others." True, Jimmie's parents should have taken more initiative in making contact with his teachers, but since they did not, at least something was accomplished through the teacher's going to them.

It is generally accepted in most church schools that teachers should visit homes. Then why are there so few who actually do it? One reason given is that teachers are too busy. This is not convincing. Except in a widely scattered parish, the time involved in making six to a dozen calls (large classes should have associate teachers who can help with the calls) is not so great that it needs to be a deterrent. One teacher who was new in the church community and who did not have a car solved this problem by getting one of the mothers to volunteer to drive her.

Another reason given is that teachers mean to make visits, but just do not get around to it. This difficulty can be met through a plan which provides that each teacher visit all homes within a week at the beginning of the church school year. At the end of the week, reports are made on visits completed. If the teachers themselves share in making such a plan, it is likely to get results.

Perhaps the most important reason for not making visits is that teachers are unsure of themselves because they do not know just what to say when they call. The following experiences suggest ways of meeting this problem: (1) In one church, the superintendent or an experienced teacher accompanied each new teacher on two or three of their first visits as a sort of demonstration, but mainly to reassure them that it was not so hard as they had thought and might even be a pleasant experience. (2) In another church, the plan for having all homes visited by teachers was related to the distribution of the parents' magazine, so that there would be a definite object in the call. Many experienced teachers make it a point always to have one definite purpose in making a call because this makes an easy point of contact, and conversation can then go to other matters as the opportunity is opened. (3) A third church built the program of one of the workers' conferences around the importance of home relationships, and demonstrated the way in which home visits might be made by means of two role-plays of such visits.

Visits to homes in behalf of the church school need not be limited to teachers, though obviously the teacher himself must make such visits if he is to get the full benefit from them. The pastor in his regular parish calling will often have opportunity to promote the interests of the church school and to deal with matters of Christian nurture in the home. This will be enhanced if the church school workers inform him of new families which have enrolled pupils, and of problem situations in which he can help. In turn, the pastor will report to the church school workers anything he learns which will be of help to them.

4. *Provide useful resource materials for parents.* The church library should have useful books and pamphlets for parents in meeting their problems in Christian nurture, as well as reading materials for children. But such materials will not be used unless parents are informed of their availability. Some churches arrange a book and pamphlet table in the foyer of the church. Some list new materials in the church bulletin or parish paper. One pastor prepared a list of helpful books for prospective parents, and arranged with a local book store to keep them in stock. Some have prepared lists of good books for children which are suitable to give as Christmas and birthday presents. One purpose of the nursery roll is to supply parents of young children with helpful reading materials through the home visitor. Some church libraries include victrola records for children which may be checked out over a period of time. Many churches have found it useful to print a prospectus of the church school program, including objectives, courses in each grade, names of officers and teachers, standards of work, desirable home cooperation, and so on, for distribution to all homes.

5. *Hold meetings for parents.* The parent-teacher meeting in the public school is well established and serves a useful purpose. Considering the partnership nature of Christian education, such meetings are even more important to the church school. These meetings may be held for the parents of a single class, for the parents of one department, or for the parents of the whole church school.

(1) A meeting for the parents of a single class serves as a good supplement to home visits, since it gives the teacher a further opportunity for intimate contact. Moreover,

when they meet as a group parents will stimulate and educate each other. It is a good plan to have such meetings in the homes, with parents acting as hosts and personally inviting the other parents in addition to the general invitation by the teacher. Such a meeting can deal with standards of work, pre-view of future lessons, evaluation of the class program with suggestions for improvement, use of home materials, reports on effectiveness from both the parents' and teacher's point of view, mutual problems. A meeting for mothers only might be held in the morning or early afternoon when children are in school, provided, of course, that the teacher is available at that time. Let us not forget, however, that fathers are also parents!

(2) The department parent-teacher meeting is practical as a means for bringing together the parents who have children of approximately the same age. If the church is using a group or departmental graded curriculum, it is also practical from the standpoint of bringing together those whose children are using the same lesson materials. A good time to hold department meetings is at the beginning of each quarter so that the program may include a pre-view of the curriculum for the quarter which lies ahead.

(3) The all-church parent meeting is useful in considering general objectives and the program as a whole, and for discussion of topics which apply to all parents. It is not practical for the consideration of topics and problems which do not apply equally to parents of children of all ages. Also, if well attended, the all-church meeting is usually too large to permit the more intimate discussion that is most appropriate for the purpose of such meetings. It is possible to combine both general and departmental or class meetings in the program for a single evening by

giving a part of the time to each type. However, when department or class meetings are held simultaneously, some parents will be confronted with the difficulty of having children in more than one department or class and having to choose between two or more groups in which they are expected to be present.

The programs for meetings of parents and teachers will vary as widely as the purposes for which they are held. These purposes will include: (1) better acquaintance of parents with teachers, and with each other; (2) opportunity for getting parents' point of view; (3) interpretation of the church school to parents; (4) consideration of problems in Christian nurture in home and church school; (5) definition of mutual responsibilities of parents and workers; (6) pre-view of curriculum and other plans by classes or departments; (7) occasion for parents, pupils, and teachers to share a pleasant experience in the church. Here are a few points to observe in planning the program:

(1) It should provide for sharing of mutual interests and problems. It is not just an opportunity for workers to exhort the parents. The group conference method is better than lectures. Maximum participation by members of the group is desirable. If speakers or audio-visuals are to be used for the presentation of special topics, these topics should grow out of local needs, and the presentations followed by discussion and application to the local situation.

(2) A spirit of good fellowship should be encouraged. A supper meeting is helpful, but parents do not like to leave their children during the evening meal. One church solved this by having a pot-luck supper for the entire family, followed by fellowship singing. Then the parents and teachers retired to another part of the building for their educational program, while the children had their

own program of movies in the dining room. Some have found that a dessert meeting, following dinner at home, helps to accomplish the purpose of fellowship, and others find it helpful to have refreshments at the end of the meeting. Personal acquaintance of parents and teachers may be facilitated by having the latter serve as hosts at tables for the parents related to their classes, or through other ways of bringing them together.

(3) Some churches have found Sunday afternoon to be a good time for meetings which also include the children. A pattern of program might be (a) family worship, parents and children together, with children taking part in leading the service; (b) a period in which classes present a program consisting of an exhibit of some of their class work, such as a dramatization, a choral reading, a set of handmade lantern slides, tape recordings of interviews held, description of field trips or other projects undertaken; (c) separate meetings for parents and children—the former for their educational program, the children for a story period, movies, or other entertainment (which may also have educational value), the program for children being in charge of persons who are not involved in the educational meeting; (d) refreshments, with parents, teachers, and children together. It is to be said for such a plan that parents may welcome something to do with their children on Sunday afternoon, and that a program in which their children participate will usually bring them. The promise of entertainment and refreshments will serve to make the children eager promoters of attendance.

(4) Audio-visuals may be effectively used to present the subject for discussion. Many good recordings, filmstrips, and motion pictures are available. Selection should be made in accordance with the purpose of the meeting. Con-

sult your denominational listing of audio-visuals, as well as catalogs of other distributors for suggestions.

(5) When supper or refreshments are to be provided, the schedule should be so planned that parents and teachers who serve or clean up will not be taken out of vital parts of the meeting. These duties may be assumed by interested persons who are not normally involved in the meeting, such as high school boys and girls or adults who do not have children in the church school.

(6) Promotion of attendance is important. The success of parent meetings is in proportion to the percentage of parents and workers who attend. Mere public announcements will not be sufficient. General letters usually are not effective. In addition to such general promotion, the invitation needs to be personalized. This can readily be accomplished if each teacher takes responsibility for inviting the parents related to his class. Both parents should be encouraged to attend. In view of the importance of these meetings, parents should be taught to give them high priority in the time budget of the family. To justify this, the program needs to be interesting, helpful, and not too long.

6. *Report pupil progress to the parents.* This will be accomplished in part through informal conversations with parents. In addition, some churches provide for formal report cards to be sent periodically to the home. The values and difficulties of such reporting have been discussed in an earlier chapter. A fuller discussion will be found in *The Better Church School* by J. L. Lobingier, pp. 85-87.

7. *Utilize family worship services, and special days.* The purpose and value of such occasions have been dealt with earlier in this book. Here it is sufficient to point out that such occasions provide an opportunity for parents and

children to participate together in a service of the church. Some parents who do not ordinarily attend church will come to services in which their children have a part. The best type of program for special days is one that grows out of what children have been learning in the church school, and this will help parents to gain insight into the nature of the curriculum and some evidence of accomplishment.

8. *Bring the parents into the church school and its work.* One way of enlisting home cooperation is to go to the parents with an interpretation of the church school program and their part in it. Another way is to bring parents into the church school.

Parents are too much inclined to think of the church school staff as a group of church people who are doing something *for* them and their children. But if Christian education is primarily a responsibility of parents, should they not rather think of the church school as an agency *through* which they may do something for themselves and their children? Should they not assume primary responsibility for the church school? If this point of view were accepted, it would follow that parents would be expected to share in the activities and work of the church school. Consider a few of the ways in which this would be worked out in practice:

(1) Parents will attend church school with their children, not just bring them. Traditionally the church school has a place for everybody, parents and other adults as well as children. Most churches maintain classes for adults, but in some parts of the country the church school is being regarded as an institution for children only. Distinct values follow when parents are active in the church school: (a) it supports the interest and morale of children, and makes it less likely that they will drop out in early adolescence;

182

(b) it stimulates the parents' own religious interest and growth; (c) it relates the parents more intimately to the work which is being done in all departments, and makes them more aware of their part in the Christian nurture of their children.

If the third of these values is to be realized, the adult groups in the church school must do more than simply engage in religious study for their own benefit. A part of their effort should be devoted to a consideration of the Christian education of their children, and how they can help in this process both through the church school and the home. There may be study groups of parents at other times than on Sunday, but there is distinct value in having the parents meet as a part of the Sunday morning church school.

(2) Parents and children may worship together in a family service. This type of service has been described on pages 108-110. The family service emphasizes the unity of Christian education with the whole church because it is not just a Sunday school session but a service of worship of the church. It is followed by class sessions for the parents as well as for children. The subject matter for these parents' classes should include help in Christian home making, and in understanding what is going on in the church school classes for children.

(3) Women's and men's groups in the church may serve as auxiliaries to the church school. Such groups usually engage in service activities of many kinds. Why should they not also give their effort to the improvement of Christian education? There are many ways in which they could be of help, such as providing transportation for field trips, serving suppers for workers' conferences and parent-teacher meetings, repairing equipment and providing needed new equipment, re-decorating rooms, helping with

enlistment of workers, financing delegates to youth conferences and summer schools, chaperoning youth activities, helping with scouting, directing and costuming plays, visiting new families. Such activities in behalf of the church school would inevitably lead to better understanding of and greater interest in Christian education.

(4) Parents will occasionally visit the departments and classes of their children in order to see the program which is being carried on. Teachers should take the initiative in inviting parents to visit. A general visiting day is not practical because experience shows that parents will not respond to a general invitation, and if a large percentage of them did come, there would be no room for them. It is better for teachers to work out a schedule of visits and invite two or four parents to be the guests of the class on a particular Sunday.

(5) Parents may serve as class sponsors. One couple at a time will be asked to serve for a period of one month or six weeks. Sponsors may attend class sessions and serve as assistants to the teacher. They may act as observers of the session and help the teacher in evaluating it. They may help with such matters as providing transportation for trips, inviting other parents and serving as hosts for class meetings of parents, providing refreshments for class parties, helping with thru-the-week meetings for class projects, distributing parents' magazines and other materials, telephoning other parents when there is need for this.

(6) Parents will accept appointment to the staff of workers in the church school. In any church, some parents will be found in the staff of workers. But if parents are primarily responsible for Christian education, why should these few do the work for all the others? Why not expect all parents to serve for at least one year in some capacity? If

this obligation were ever taken seriously, there would be less difficulty in recruiting church school workers!

There are objections to such a plan. Not all parents are suited to be teachers. This objection can be met to some extent. If what they lack is experience and training, a training program could be instituted which would prepare some for future service while others are doing the active work. If their lack is one of inclination or temperament to serve as teachers, such persons might undertake some of the other numerous jobs that need doing.

Another objection is that there are times when some parents are not free to undertake service in the church school. They may have other church responsibilities, they may be too completely occupied with young children in the home, or there may be other situations which make them unavailable. Such persons may become available at some future time, and may plan ahead for taking their place when they are able to do so.

A third objection is that it is not possible to build a competent staff with people who expect to serve for one year only. This is a valid objection. There must be a core of those who make the church school their primary interest over a period of years. General officers, department principals, teachers of training classes, and other key workers must be recruited from persons who regard their church school service as something more than a year's enlistment. In other words, some will always need to carry a larger responsibility for the church school than others, and because of their interest and special talents will be glad to do so. Nevertheless, the assumption that parents are primarily responsible for the church school, once accepted by them, could do wonders for the educational program of the church.

BRINGING THE CHURCH SCHOOL TO THE HOME

Not everyone can attend the church school. For those who cannot attend, the church school may be brought to their homes. There are two agencies for doing this.

1. *The Nursery Roll,* also called the Cradle Roll, ministers to babies before they are old enough to attend, and more particularly to their parents. A nursery roll superintendent and her helpers (visitors) enroll babies as soon as possible after they are born. They visit the homes periodically, send birthday cards, distribute literature which will help parents to take the first steps in Christian nurture, and arrange meetings for parents. As soon as the child is of an age for which provision is made in the church school, parents are encouraged to bring him for the sessions, and his name is then transferred to the attending membership list. The nursery roll provides an effective plan for contacts with homes and for recruiting members.

2. *The Home Department* provides home study for those who for any reason cannot attend the sessions of the church school, such as illness, infirmity, or Sunday work. A superintendent and his helpers make systematic visits to members, and bring them the study quarterlies. If a tape recorder is available, they may take recordings of the minister's sermon to shut-ins. Those who are temporarily prevented from attending the church school are encouraged to return as soon as possible.

Materials for home study are provided by publishers of lesson materials as a regular part of the church school curriculum. Similarly, supplies and other helps for the nursery roll and home department superintendents are made available.

Some churches provide an extension service by keeping in contact with young people who are away at college or in the armed services, and others who are away from home.

The nursery roll and home department may be organizationally related to the Sunday school, or they may operate directly under the committee on Christian education and thus represent the church school as a whole. Members should be counted in the total constituency served by the church school but excluded from any figures on which percentages of attendance are based.

11 THE ENLISTMENT
OF WORKERS

A superintendent had a dream. He dreamed that all the problems of a working staff for his church school, problems which had caused him many a wakeful hour of worry, had been solved. This is what he saw in his dream: He had a group of associate general officers who knew their jobs and were enthusiastically performing them. He had a principal for every department, competently doing his work, with the help of a good pianist and other needed departmental workers, and eager to coordinate the work of his department with that of the whole school. Every class had a competent teacher, and for larger classes there were also associate teachers. Men as well as women were serving throughout the church school, including the pre-school department. These workers all had designated substitutes to call on when needed, but they were rarely called on because the workers themselves found surprisingly few occasions for absence.

188

On any Sunday, these workers were all present 15 minutes before opening time, and some of them earlier. Their work for the day was planned, and they were eager to get on with it. They had prepared themselves for their work through reading, conferences, and training classes, but none felt that they had already attained. They were anxious to improve their work. When workers' conferences were held, they could be relied on to be present without coercion. They availed themselves of the community training school and other training opportunities.

Besides the regular staff there were persons in reserve, ready to take the place of any who might find it necessary to resign. There were training classes in which young people and others were preparing for future service. Everything was as it should be. . . .

But then he woke up, and all his problems were still roosting on the foot of his bed.

THE NO. 1 PROBLEM

A bulletin published by a denominational board of Christian education bears the title: *Our Number 1 Problem: Leadership.* Ninety-nine percent of pastors and superintendents will probably agree with this, as also with the two sentences which follow: "There is no problem confronting the church that is weighted with greater importance than that of developing a consecrated, trained leadership. The success or failure of all enterprises in the life and work of every church is determined more by the character and quality of the leaders giving direction to those enterprises than by any other factor."[1]

Of all the superintendents who wrote to make suggestions for this book, only one stated "At the present time we

---

[1] Board of Christian Education, Presbyterian Church in the U.S.A.

have enough leaders and teachers," but even he wisely added, "How can we train younger persons to take over in later years?" Almost all others asked for help on some phase of the problems of workers: How do we find persons who are willing to serve? How do we get them to take training? How can we motivate them to do their work faithfully? How do we get rid of those who are not effective?

Any author who can give a simple formula by which the problems of leadership will be solved should be nominated for a Church School Hall of Fame. We know no easy answers. We know only that careful planning, perseverance, and consecrated efforts will get results.

ARE PROFESSIONAL WORKERS THE ANSWER?

Can we ever have good Christian education with lay workers? Are we undertaking a task so complex, so difficult, so awesomely important, that only those who have professional training and are paid to give the necessary time can hope to accomplish it? Roman Catholics and Jews have answered this second question in the affirmative. This has resulted in two types of schools for religious education: (1) the religious day school, or parochial school, which places all education under religious auspices and includes the teaching of the Bible, the catechism, and other specific religious materials; (2) a religious school meeting after public school for one to three days a week, and sometimes with the addition of a long Sunday morning session. Even when they have a Sunday session only, Jewish congregations devote three hours to it and employ professionally trained teachers.

The Protestant church approaches this latter type of school in the church membership or confirmation class in charge of the pastor, the weekday church school, and the vacation church school when it is staffed by employed, professional workers (which is not usually the case). Primarily, the Protestant church maintains its faith in a church school with voluntary workers. Most churches will not change from this plan, for the following reasons:

1. Protestants believe too strongly in the public school to be willing to withdraw their children from it in favor of a religious day school.

2. The cost of employing a faculty for either type of school would be prohibitive for most congregations, nor would they be able to find the necessary number of professional teachers.

3. It is questionable whether the influence of the Protestant church with most families is strong enough to assure the enrollment of a considerable percentage of children in an extensive after-school program. (This statement may be too pessimistic. Perhaps much more could be done along this line.)

4. The Protestant conception of the nature of Christian education is such as to require that it be given in the followship of the church by the people of the church, rather than *for* the church by a professional staff.

Nevertheless, we believe that the church school will never be as effective as it should without the ministry of someone who has the training of a professional worker and the time which can be given only by one employed for this work. Under the guidance of such a worker, a voluntary staff can be recruited and trained to do effective work; without it we are likely to continue to have the kind of church schools that have brought the very word "Sunday school" into disrepute.

Does this leave most churches in a hopeless situation?

By no means. In most churches the minister can and must give this professional service. His responsibility is to the whole church, and this includes the church school. If he is not trained in Christian education, his training has been faulty. If he is not devoting a part of his time to Christian education, he is derelict in his duty. Some stronger churches can add a minister of Christian education to the employed staff. Some have a lay person in their membership who has sufficient training to direct the work in Christian education, in cooperation with the minister. In such cases, less will be required of the minister, but Christian education is such a vital part of the life and work of the church that he will still be very much concerned with it.

One source of professional leadership that is available to most churches but too little used is the educational and field staffs of the denominations and councils of churches. Their services are given through published leaflets and bulletins, conferences, correspondence, and personal visits. They cannot supply the need for continuous professional leadership in each church but can give an occasional impetus to better work and expert guidance on particular problems. Local churches will do well to make judicious use of these staff leaders.

LAY WORKERS MUST DO IT

For the Protestant church, the plan of committing Christian education largely to lay workers is not simply an economic necessity. It is also the soundest way of accomplishing its purpose. This follows from the nature of the church.

1. The church is a redemptive and educational influence because it is a fellowship of young and old in a common purpose. The more mature share their faith with the less mature as together they seek more fully to know

and to do God's will. Just as a Christian family cannot assign its function in Christian nurture to a nurse or governess, so a church cannot leave its work in Christian education to a professional staff. While the church school must partake of the nature of a school, it is most effective when it also has the nature of a family, with the more mature Christians taking the role of parents. The doctrine of the "priesthood of all believers" makes every member a teacher as well as a learner. The Christian faith is caught as well as taught, and both these elements are inseparably combined in its communication. While it utilizes the methods which are necessary to all good teaching, Christian education places a premium on the person who teaches, and is concerned that he be first of all a dynamic, living witness.

2. The church is dedicated not only to the worship of God and the hearing of his Word, but also to Christian work in his name. All members should expect to be about their Father's business. They must take literally the admonition "Bear ye one another's burdens." Recognizing with Paul (Eph. 4:11) that there is diversity of gifts, each should be willing to render the ministry that he is able to render. Some because of aptitude and inclination will be called to be teachers, while others can better minister in other ways. The church has not only the right but also the obligation to call its members into voluntary service, and should expect a response which is joyously and not grudgingly given.

3. While teaching is a complex and difficult art, its essentials can be mastered by lay workers who have the inclination to do so. The necessary preparation will not be taken lightly by those who have a deep conviction concerning the importance of what they are called to do.

4. Service in the church school gives an opportunity

for parents to share in providing Christian nurture for their children in an organized program which has its primary base in the home. It is an effective way of linking the church and home in a process which can fully succeed only when both are involved in it.

5. Sharing in Christian education is a means of stimulating the development of Christian faith and life in the workers themselves. It is a characteristic of the Christian faith that the more it is confessed and shared, the more it grows. It would be a great loss to the people of the church if the responsibility for Christian education were taken away from them.

WHY A PROBLEM?

In face of the above considerations, why should it be a problem to get workers for the church school?

1. One reason is that churches fall short of being what a Christian church ought to be. Their members are not fully committed to discipleship. To enlist consecrated workers in such a situation is like trying to gather figs from thorns or grapes from bramble bushes (Luke 6:44). What is needed first is re-dedication of the congregation to be a church in the full sense. By one method or another such commitment to the central purpose of the church must be achieved if we are not to deserve the fate of the barren fig tree (Luke 13:6-9).

An example of one approach to this problem is what has been done by many Episcopal churches in relation to the adoption of a new curriculum. This is the parish life conference, usually conducted as a week-end retreat. Key persons of the church are invited to these conferences, to review and evaluate present program, with a view to re-studying the nature and purpose of the church and look-

ing toward a new dedication to its true mission. It is anticipated that once the new spirit has been caught by an inner
group of leaders it will radiate out to others.

2. A second reason why we have this problem of leadership is that churches are not Christian-education conscious.
Most churches have a Sunday school, and would not be
without it. But beyond this, most members know or care
little about what these schools are actually doing. As long
as they are not bothered by the children, and no great
demands are made on the budget, they are willing to leave
all such matters to the superintendent and his staff. They
should not be blamed for this attitude if no effort has
been made to educate the congregation on the importance
of Christian education. If ministers do not speak out in its
behalf, if official boards do not give it a place in their
concern, if parents are not made aware of its significance,
the church school will continue to hold a place of minor
importance. Under these circumstances, no one should
be surprised that it is difficult to recruit a working staff.

3. A third reason for the problem is the way in which
it is usually handled. This is the "hand to mouth" method
of trying to fill vacancies when they occur, without systematic planning for the future. It has resulted in some positions going unfilled for weeks at a time, various organizations competing with each other for the few available
workers, some persons being overworked while others
avoid responsibility, inadequate performance of duties because of lack of preparation for them, and rapid turnover
of personnel. What is needed is a long-range plan which
brings three factors into focus: (1) a study of the need for
leadership throughout the church, (2) a canvass of the
constituency to discover those who are best fitted to fill the
places, (3) a systematic plan for enlistment and training.

ENLISTMENT OF WORKERS

It is one of the duties of the committee on Christian education to recruit, appoint, and train the workers. If the church does not have such a committee, or if it is not active, the minister and superintendent will need to assume this responsibility. In any case they will need to work closely with the committee because (1) the minister knows the people of the parish better than anyone else, and (2) the superintendent is most aware of positions which need to be filled.

The committee as a whole can develop policies, make plans, and approve recommendations for appointment. The detailed work will need to be assigned to a smaller sub-committee and individuals. For a long-range plan, it is suggested that there be a committee on personnel to work continuously at the job. Ideally, one committee should deal with the problem of leadership for the whole church, but since this book is directed to the church school we shall limit our discussion to Christian education leadership.

1. *Where shall prospects be found?* With few exceptions, the workers must be found among the members of the congregation. This is inherent in our plan for a voluntary staff. Most churches have in their membership sufficient talent to provide a staff for their church schools, if only they can be enlisted and trained. These same people are the parents of the children in the church school and the responsible leaders of the church. Surely the best among them are also fit to be workers in the church school. If this faith in the vitality of the Christian fellowship is not justified, then the church is incapable of maintaining and perpetuating itself.

2. *What qualifications are required?* Workers are chosen

for what they are and for what they can do. (1) Those who are to lead others into discipleship, will of necessity themselves be sincere, dedicated Christians, who believe in the church and its work. They are living witnesses to the faith they teach, in deeds as well as in words. They should be persons who gladly serve because they love the Lord and love the people with whom they work. (2) Each worker must have competence to do the work for which he is called. The qualities and skills required will vary with different positions, but will include: sufficient general education to handle the curriculum, understanding of pupils, executive and administrative ability, ability to communicate, sufficient maturity to lead others, knowledge of the subject to be taught, skill in teaching and in the processes of group leadership, willingness to learn. Most of these can be acquired through training, and improved by experience.

The list of qualifications for leadership could easily be extended, but to do so would put us in danger of "pricing ourselves out of the market." Nor would it serve a useful purpose. In any church those responsible for personnel will have the necessary qualifications in mind and then seek to enlist the most capable persons they can find. The qualities of personality and character which make any person a successful worker cannot readily be analyzed into a list of specific traits. Nor can all workers be molded in a single pattern. Each must make his contribution through the talents with which he has been endowed, the abilities which he has acquired, and the skills which he is able to learn and practice.

Whether the workers be men or women usually makes no great difference, because other factors are more important. In this connection it should be noted, however, that the common practice of having only women work with younger children is not desirable. It is better to have some men in the staff at all age levels, including pre-school children. If the case were reversed, and there were a tendency for men rather than women to fill the positions, we would make the same stipulation for women throughout the school. We are favorably impressed with the increasing tendency to enlist couples as co-teachers. It offers them an interesting activity to share, gives the class the benefit of having both male and female leadership, and obviates the need for a substitute when one has to be absent.

Should high school boys and girls be used as teachers? They may serve as assistants and helpers, but only the most mature are ready at this age to be teachers. While it is desirable to give boys and girls experience in service activities, this should not deprive them of continuing their own Christian education in classes and youth groups.

3. *How motivate for service?* The only adequate motivation to service is willing response to God's love and grace. Discipleship implies Christian work. It has been emphasized earlier that unless the spirit of the church supports this attitude there is no adequate solution to its problems of leadership. Whether this "call" finds its outlet in service in the church school or in some other field depends on such factors as (1) Does this person realize the need for Christian education and the importance of the church school in all that the church stands for? (2) Does he feel that he has a responsibility for helping to meet this need, as a parent or as a member of the church? (3) Is he aware that he has certain interests and abilities which make him capable of contributing something of value in meeting this need?

Individual interests and capacities will provide more

specific motivation for service in the church school. Some persons find satisfaction in working with children or young people. Some have a "knack" for teaching. Some like the executive work involved in serving as officers. Some gain satisfaction from being associated with others in a worthy cause. Some parents respond to the opportunity of helping to improve the church school for their children's sake, or just the obligation to do their share. All such motivations can be used to the glory of God.

The approach to the enlistment of prospective workers will assume that they are committed to Christian work and expect to take their share in the service of the church. It will emphasize the importance of Christian education. and the particular contribution which the prospect can make. It will stress opportunity rather than obligation. If obligation is emphasized, it will be obligation to God and the church, not just to a group of workers who need help. High pressure salesmanship is not desirable, for a reluctant or unwilling recruit will often prove to be a hindrance rather than a help.

4. *What should be the term of service?* Annual appointment of the church school staff is a good plan. Some will agree to serve for one year when they would not be willing to commit themselves for a longer period. Those who are not giving satisfactory service can more easily be removed if their appointment expires at a definite time. Annual appointment assumes, of course, that many will be reappointed at the end of the year. If the desire for self-improvement is present, competence should improve with length of service. Some may give most of their lives to service in the church school because of interest in and competence for this phase of the church's work. It is not possible to have an effective staff without a hard core of

perennials who have given the church school an important place in their lives. On the other hand, there is value in spreading work in Christian education widely among the members of the church rather than leaving it too much to a "faithful few."

Should workers be given a leave of absence from time to time? It seems reasonable that anyone who has served for a period of years should be allowed an interim year of rest from church school activity. Usually this is at the option of the worker, since there seems to be no way to compel anyone to continue serving against his will. Some schools which are well staffed are making it a policy to provide a "sabbatical" year for everyone after three or more years of continuous service.

5. *What plan should be used for enlistment?* It has been suggested that there be a committee on personnel to deal with the enlistment and training of workers on a long-range basis. This committee might proceed with its work as follows:

(1) Plan for a continuous program of leadership development, looking forward to the future as well as meeting the present need. When immediate needs have been met, continue to enlist and train a corps of reserves.

(2) Study the work of the whole church school to determine what kind of positions need to be filled, and the qualifications required.

(3) Make a canvass of the people of the church to determine who may be available for service, either immediately or in the future. Keep a card file on each person listed, indicating personal data, qualifications, training and experience, type of service for which best suited, age-group interest, record of interviews, and so on. Once this file is made, keep it up to date by adding new persons who join

the church, and young people as they become mature enough for leadership positions.

How soon may new members of the church properly be included as prospects? There is no good reason why they should not be included at once. If they are committed to the purpose and work of the church, they are usually ready to take their places in its service. The sooner they can be enlisted, the less likely it will be that they will have assumed other responsibilities.

(4) Educate the church on the importance of Christian education and the need for workers. This can be done through sermons on Christian education, the church news letter, Christian Education Week and other special programs, home visits, interpretation of the work of the church school in other agencies of the church. The confirmation reunion service is an opportunity to emphasize re-dedication to Christian service, with particular reference to Christian nurture in home and church school. Such approaches are to prepare the way for personal interviews. They should not include a general invitation for volunteers.

(5) Select those who are to be invited to leadership positions, and extend the call to them. Some churches have successfully used a letter of invitation to service, issued in the name of the committee on Christian education. A form prepared for this purpose is reproduced on page 202 by courtesy of the Board of Parish Education of the Norwegian Lutheran Church.

A more effective method is to have the call extended in a personal interview. It is usually best for two persons who are already active in the program to make the call. The visitors should explain the work of the church school, and answer any questions concerning it. They will make clear that Christian education is the concern of the whole

A Letter of Call for Parish Church School Teachers

IN THE NAME OF THE FATHER AND OF THE SON AND OF THE HOLY GHOST

The Board of Parish Education of...Lutheran Church believes that you are qualified both spiritually and intellectually for teaching in the Kingdom of God, and hereby extends to you, ..., a call to serve your Lord and Savior, Jesus Christ, by teaching ....in the.......................church school.
(grade or class)

The Board believes that you will by the grace of God:

Give of your best in this service, remembering that faithfulness to the assigned task is the supreme virtue in the kingdom.

Read God's Word daily and pray earnestly for your pupils as well as for yourself as a teacher.

Worship regularly with the congregation on Sunday except when prevented by sickness or other reasons which you can conscientiously take before your God.

Teach the Word of God as found in the sacred Scriptures and the accepted textbooks, and in harmony with the interpretation and the teachings of the Lutheran Church.

Seek constantly to improve your teaching by good lesson preparation, private study, and regular attendance at teacher-training classes and monthly teachers' meetings.

Attend Sunday school every Sunday and if, for unavoidable reasons, you must be absent or tardy, that you will make the necessary arrangements with your superintendent or associate.

Lead in public and in private a life that is worthy of the holy office to which you have been called.

Give diligence to present thyself approved unto God, a workman that needeth not to be ashamed, handling aright the Word of Truth. II Timothy 2:15.

_____, 19____.   On behalf of the Board of Parish Education

_____ Chairman

_____ Secretary

Having prayerfully considered the above call, and being conscious of my many shortcomings but loving my Savior and trusting in His grace, help, and guidance, I hereby accept the call to teach....................................in the
(grade or class)
...................................Church School of...........................Lutheran Church for the school year..................

Signed _____

Address _____

Telephone_____

church, and of every member. If no more than this is accomplished the visit will have been worth making. At least one person or family will be better informed because of it. It may even happen that at this point the visitors will decide that it would be unwise for this person to accept appointment, and not press the invitation.

Normally the interview will next proceed to a definite invitation to the prospect to accept a position in the church school staff, with a description of the position that he is to fill, his qualifications for it, and the responsibilities that are involved. This job description should be clearly covered, without making it too simple and easy. Most persons will respond better to a job which calls for the best they can give than one that requires little of them. Here is an opportunity to get the new worker started off with the right attitude toward his work. If the visitors themselves are enthusiastic about their own work in the church school, this will be contagious. If the prospect protests that he is not capable, remind him that all the workers are volunteers and most of them had to learn on the job. Assure him that help is available in curriculum materials, training conferences, and counsel with the minister, superintendent, and department principal.

If a favorable answer is received, arrangements should be made for a conference with the superintendent or department principal in which the curriculum material will be delivered and explained and other duties of the new office interpreted. If the prospect is not ready to reach a decision, recognize the need for due consideration on his part and arrange for a subsequent interview. If it becomes clear that he cannot now accept, leave the way open to renew the invitation another year.

(6) Some persons can be drawn into the staff of workers

by first letting them try themselves in minor positions. They may be willing to serve as assistant teachers or class observers. They may get their start as parent sponsors to classes. Thus they can learn much about teaching by observing what a more experienced teacher is doing, and begin to get the feel of working with a group of pupils.

(7) Not all prospective workers need to be recruited by this formal process. Some will respond to a more casual invitation. Some may even volunteer to serve. But for a systematic plan of enlistment this more elaborate procedure is recommended. The importance of the tasks to be undertaken justifies the effort needed to make the call to service dignified and forceful.

(8) The usual policy is to appoint teachers to a given age or grade, and to let them remain in that grade year after year, while classes are promoted to higher grades. This enables them to become reasonably expert with that age of pupil, and if graded lessons are used, to become thoroughly familiar with one year of the curriculum. Sometimes shifts to older or younger pupils are desirable because it is discovered that the teacher has more aptitude with another age-group. It is good for classes to have a change of teacher each year so as to get the benefit of contact with a variety of personalities. If under unusual circumstances it becomes desirable to promote a teacher with his class, he may stay with them through their three years in one department, but after that return to a younger class in the same department.

INDUCTION INTO SERVICE

It is important that new workers get the proper start in their work. The transition from appointment to active service will be made easier if the following steps are taken:

1. *Interpretation of the Job.* A clear understanding of duties and relationships should be given the new worker. The process may be begun in the interview when he is invited to serve, and continued through subsequent conferences with church school officers. This is the time to emphasize and interpret the need for regular attendance, procedure in providing for a substitute in case of necessary absence, regular lesson preparation, attendance at workers' conferences and other training sessions, cooperation with the secretary in keeping accurate records, how to get equipment and supplies, resources available in the church library. If any published guides are available, such as a manual of procedure or standards for teachers, these should be interpreted at this time.

2. *Pre-service Training.* It would be good if every new worker could take a course of training before entering on his duties. When this cannot be done, he should at least be given his curriculum materials as early as possible, and make a preview of them. Their use should be carefully explained. If necessary, help should be given in preparing teaching plans for the first few sessions. Much of this might well be accomplished in a workers' retreat at the beginning of the church school year.

3. *Introduction to Fellow Workers and Pupils.* Prior to beginning service, a teacher should be given a list of names, addresses, and telephone numbers of pupils in his class. A new department principal should have similar data on the other officers and teachers in the department. When a new teacher is to replace one who has resigned, it is helpful if there can be an overlap of a Sunday or two during which he may observe. On his first Sunday a new worker should be properly introduced by the department principal or general superintendent.

4. *Consecration of Workers.* An annual church service of commissioning in which all workers are introduced to the congregation and consecrated to their work is highly desirable. The following simple ritual of commissioning was used in a family service. It was preceded by a sermon on Christian education.

THE SERVICE OF COMMISSIONING

The members of the church school staff will come before the chancel as they are introduced by the minister.

Minister: Jesus said, "You did not choose me,
but I chose you and appointed you
that you should go and bear fruit and
that your fruit should abide."

Staff: We ask God's help that our labor
may bear fruit, for without him
we can do nothing.

Minister: "And his gifts were that some should
be apostles, some prophets, some
evangelists, some pastors and teachers,
for building up the body of Christ."

Staff: Unto thee, O Lord, do we lift up our
souls. Show us thy ways, O Lord; teach
us thy paths, and lead us in thy truth.

Minister: Charge to the Staff
Charge to the Congregation
Prayer of Consecration

Hymn of Consecration: "Lord, Speak to Me that I May
Speak" (Canonbury)

Other suggested commissioning services may be found in the booklet ". . . And Gladly Serve," published by the National Council of Churches, Division of Christian Education, and in the September issues of some Christian education journals.

5. *Continuing Support.* New workers especially should have the support of the officers of the church school, expressed in interest in their work and help given in meeting the first difficulties which arise. The first weeks are the most important in developing good workers.

TERMINATION OF SERVICE

Most workers resign from their jobs all too soon. Yet in every discussion of leadership problems someone is almost sure to ask, "How do you get rid of workers who are not effective?"

It is probably inevitable that some mistakes are made in appointments. These mistakes can be reduced to a minimum if pre-service training is provided, and if new workers are given an opportunity to try themselves as observers, assistants, substitutes, or in temporary appointments. Getting rid of ineffective workers is rarely a problem once the committee on Christian education is in charge of leadership and keeps the matter under constant study and control. A plan for annual appointments is helpful because it is easier not to re-appoint an ineffective worker than to ask him to resign. Those who are not making a success of their work will usually recognize this in the course of the year and decline re-appointment.

Unfortunately, the persons in question usually have been in service for a long time and do not recognize the necessity for re-appointment. In dealing with them we must regard their feelings as well as the welfare of the church school, and avoid as much as possible doing them an injury. In most cases the following approaches to the problem will work:

1. Annual appointment of all workers by the committee on Christian education. This not only enhances the

importance and dignity of the appointments, but also makes the transaction less personal.

2. Provision for a training program, with insistence that all workers participate in it. The best way to eliminate a poor worker is to make a better one out of him. It is easier to keep people from getting into a rut than to get them out of it.

3. Establishment and maintenance of high standards for workers. This may cause the ineffective ones to improve, or to eliminate themselves because they realize that they no longer fit.

4. Flexibility in making assignments to jobs. Sometimes a person who is not so good at one thing may be able to do something else satisfactorily.

5. Patience, forbearance, and charity in dealing with persons. Time has a way of solving problems. This, however, must not be carried to the point of weakness or cowardice. When the welfare of pupils is at stake, those responsible for the church school must take steps to protect them. When drastic steps must be taken, let it be done in love and with a frank facing of the facts by all concerned.

SUBSTITUTE TEACHERS

Unavoidable absences of workers are almost sure to occur. What is the best way to provide for substitutes in such cases?

1. If the plan of having co-teachers, or a head teacher with an assistant, is followed, there is no problem. One of them will usually be available.

2. Another good plan is for each teacher to have a designated substitute on whom he may call. The teacher will share with this substitute his plans for the class, provide

him with the teaching materials and encourage him to become familiar with them, and invite him to visit the class occasionally in order to get acquainted with the pupils and the class procedure. Such a prepared substitute can go into action even on short notice.

3. A less effective plan is to have a list of substitutes for the church school or for each department. The teacher should inform the principal as early as possible of an impending absence. The principal should secure the substitute and inform the teacher. It then becomes the teacher's duty to have a conference with the substitute in order to supply him with the lesson materials and brief him on what should be accomplished in the session. Teachers should be sufficiently aware of the unfortunate effect on a class of even one absence to be willing to make the necessary effort to have the best possible substitution. It makes for an intolerable situation if teachers absent themselves without notice, thus forcing the principal to impress some unprepared person into service, or combining two classes for the day.

12 THE TRAINING OF WORKERS

Training is essential to effective Christian service. If church schools were conducted by professional workers, we might expect them to be trained before they are called into service. Depending as it does on voluntary workers, the church must assume responsibility for training them. A training program is an important part of the curriculum of Christian education.

1. A training program can succeed only to the extent that workers feel a need for self-improvement. The right attitude toward training should grow out of the commitment of each worker to do the best of which he is capable because he senses the importance of his job. Every church school worker might well take 2 Timothy 2:15 as his watchword: "Do your best to present yourself to God as one approved, a workman who has no need to be ashamed, rightly handling the word of truth." The right attitude toward participating in training should be emphasized at

the time when a worker is interviewed for appointment. It may be further developed through the use of standards for workers, and contagious contact with other workers who are eagerly seeking self-improvement.

2. A second requirement for success of a training program is ample opportunity for training. We must bear in mind that we are dealing with lay men and women who have many other obligations. It would be wonderful if every member of the staff were always available when training meetings are called. This is not usually the case. Hence it is necessary to provide a variety of opportunities for training to fit the convenience of the workers. Moreover, not all workers are at the same stage of development, and this makes it necessary to have different types of training activities as well as to provide for individual guidance. Those responsible for training should therefore be prepared to shape the training program to meet the situations and needs of the workers, and should also expect the workers to make some concession in their own convenience so as to be able to take advantage of what is offered. An important group conference which some workers are unable to attend may well be followed by individual conferences with those who are absent so as to give them some of the benefits from the conference.

3. Most of the training opportunities are provided by the local church for its own workers. Others are made available for the churches of a community and wider areas by the denominations and councils of churches. Local church leaders should make the best possible use of both.

OBJECTIVES OF TRAINING

Everyone appointed for service brings with him a certain amount of preparation. He has many years of general education. He has usually had some years of Christian education in the church school and the general program of the church. He may have had experience in business or profession. If he is a parent, he has had intimate contacts with children. Without this background our task of training would be hopeless. To this general background there must be added some training for Christian education, varying somewhat with the duties to be performed, but including at least the following for each worker:

1. Opportunity for growth in personal faith and attitudes, through study, devotional practices, and deepening of commitment.

2. Understanding of the nature and purpose of Christian education in general, and of his own church school and its work in particular.

3. Understanding of the process of education, how learning takes place, the nature and characteristics of the age of pupils with whom he works.

4. Knowledge of the subject matter that he is to teach —the Bible, church history, social issues, and so on.

5. Knowledge of the teaching techniques which are appropriate for the age of pupils with whom he works, and skill in using a variety of methods; ability to translate purpose, content, and method into an appropriate and effective session plan.

6. Development of the attitudes of good staff relationship, which will result in faithfulness, good workmanship, and cooperation.

Each of these items might easily be analyzed into many specifics. It is a large order. It will never be accomplished completely. But some approach to it must be made if we are to have good work.

PRE-SERVICE TRAINING

Some training should be given before workers actually undertake their duties. Here are a few ways in which this may be done:

1. Children and young people may be helped to develop their service interest and leadership capacities through serving as officers, committee members, program participants, and in other ways in the program of the church school department, youth groups, and vacation church school.

2. Young people should be sent to conferences, and especially summer conferences, to help deepen their Christian commitment and acquire basic training for leadership. Following such an experience, they should have the opportunity not only to report on it, but also to utilize the training that they have received. All too often they return with a new vision only to find that the home church makes no use of what they have to offer.

3. Prospective workers may gain some training and experience by serving as assistants to more seasoned leaders. Those who have such assistants assigned to them should make full use of the contribution they can make and take responsibility for helping them to learn the art of leadership.

4. The senior high and young peoples' departments of the church school may offer elective leadership training courses as a part of the regular curriculum, to encourage young people to prepare for future leadership.

5. Training classes may be held, either on Sunday morning or on weekdays, for the benefit of prospective new workers who would like to prepare themselves for service. It is especially important that new workers for the subsequent year be enlisted early enough so that a training

course may be set up for them before they begin their work.

6. While opportunity to attend summer training schools is usually reserved for those already in service, it might be very effective to have some new workers take this training before they begin their service.

7. Young people in college might be encouraged to prepare themselves for voluntary service in the church by taking courses in religion and Christian education.

IN-SERVICE TRAINING

Most of the workers in the church school begin their service without previous training. Those who have had pre-service preparation need to continue their training in relation to the jobs they undertake. Hence there is a need for a comprehensive in-service training program in every church school.

In-service training takes advantage of a sound principle of education, namely, that learning is most effective when it is related to experience. The worker's job provides the life-situation, and his need for help in doing it provides the motivation for learning. In-service training may vary from informal guidance of individual workers as they need help on specific problems, through group conferences, to formal courses. It is one of the most significant elements of a successful educational program.

1. *Starting New Teachers.* The most opportune time to begin the training of workers is when they are first appointed. One of our correspondents has asked that we give a list of do's and don'ts which may be used in guiding a new teacher. At the risk of repeating what is said elsewhere, we offer such a list in the following pages. Perhaps this will interest experienced workers as well as novices.

DO'S AND DON'TS FOR NEW TEACHERS

DO:	DO NOT:
1. Before beginning to teach,	
a. Become familiar with the curriculum as a whole, and with the unit which you are to teach.	Start with the first lesson without understanding the course as a whole.
b. Get information about your class: names, addresses, telephones, and other available data about the members and their families.	Leave this until some later time; you need it most right at the start.
c. If possible, visit the class for one Sunday before beginning your work with them.	Go into a class situation without knowing in advance something of what you may expect.
2. On your first Sunday,	
a. Introduce yourself to your class; write your name for them to see, and tell something about yourself. Identify your pupils by name.	Be just a "teacher" and not a person; identify pupils by pointing to them or otherwise offending their sense of individual personality.
b. Get off to a good start with a well-prepared lesson. Plan to keep the pupils busy, and make it interesting for them. Assume that the pupils are for you, and will be your friends if you are a friend to them.	Assume that the first session is not important; that the pupils are against you.

DO:	DO NOT:
3. Make long-range plans; roughly prepare a block of 3 or 4 lessons at a time. This will allow time to secure pictures, paper, and other needed material.	Prepare too little and too late, leaving no time to digest the material or make plans in advance.
4. Prepare for each session intensively by reading all the material in the teacher's and pupil's books, and other resources; start this early in the week. Select a few important emphases that best fit your class, and make a written plan for the session.	Try to cover everything in the lesson material; teach "off the cuff" without preparation; follow your session plan slavishly.
5. Arrive early enough on Sunday morning to see that the room is in order, all materials ready, and to greet the earliest pupils.	Rush in breathlessly at the last moment, or a few minutes late.
6. See that the room is properly arranged, clean and ventilated; that you and your pupils are comfortable, with hats and coats removed and hung in a proper place.	Accept the situation as you find it; give the impression of casual unconcern by wearing outdoor wraps or allowing pupils to do so; allow pupils to pile hats and coats on class tables.
7. Arrange seating to suit the type of method you plan to use; assign seats to individual pupils in the best interest of good order.	Permit pupils to sit in helter-skelter fashion just as they please.

DO:	DO NOT:
8. Work *with* pupils, not *for* them; let them share in planning and activity. Keep them busy with answering questions, discussion, reading, writing, dramatizing, and other activities related to the lesson.	Do everything yourself; expect pupils just to sit and listen.
9. Insist on good order, in a firm but friendly manner.	Shout, scold, or use sarcasm, or assume that if you let them do as they please pupils will like you and the class better.
10. Expect honest work from your pupils; make assignments clear, and expect that they will be done.	Assume that you cannot get pupils to do serious work; make assignments and then do not check on them, or do nothing if they are not fulfilled.
11. Be present regularly. Help find someone who will be your particular substitute when you must be absent, give him a set of the lesson materials, keep him informed on what you are doing, and occasionally have him observe your procedure.	Be absent when it can be avoided; let the superintendent know on Sunday morning that you cannot come, or worse still, send no word at all.
12. Seek home cooperation; visit the home of each pupil as soon as possible; assume that the parents are interested.	Complain about noncooperation of parents when you have done nothing to win their interest.

DO:	DO NOT:
13. Cooperate with officers in the interest of the whole school; give them a chance to help you.	Treat your job as if it had no relation to anyone else.
14. Take advantage of opportunities to improve your work —reading, teachers' meetings, training classes, and so on.	Assume that you are good enough and do not need further training.

2. *Personal Guidance*. There are numerous opportunities to help individual workers through personal counseling. When they are first appointed, they should be carefully instructed in their work. Further help may be given as they confront problems of Bible interpretation, answering religious questions, lesson planning, methods of teaching, discipline. New resources may be called to their notice. Helpful articles in magazines and chapters in books may be recommended to them when these are pertinent to their problems. Workers should feel free to seek such help from the minister, superintendent, and other competent leaders, and these should make it easy for workers to approach them by taking the initiative in discussing their work with them.

A systematic plan for personal guidance may be worked out. This would include scheduled conferences by leaders with individual workers, preceded or followed by a visit to their departments or classes. At times the help most needed is with the worker's own religious problems or his understanding of the material to be taught; it may be with planning for class sessions, or with use of specific methods, or with certain pupils, or with making home contacts. A friendly and cooperative relation must of course exist between counselor and worker. The counselor should never take the attitude that he knows all the answers, but rather that together he and the worker may find some answers.

3. *Guided Reading.* Abundant resources are available for self-training through reading. The problem is that of bringing together the worker and his need and the printed resource that will help to meet that need.

For every worker, the basic resource is the curriculum material supplied for the church school. Good curriculum material includes not only teaching material and method for each session, but also guidance in understanding the meaning of Christian education, general help in understanding the subject matter to be taught, and help in understanding pupils. The proper use of the curriculum materials is an important element in the training of workers.

Next in importance is the use of good magazines on Christian education. An example is the *International Journal of Religious Education.* Similar publications are provided by most denominations, as well as magazines directed to the work of specific age-groups. Such publications should be readily available to workers, either through individual subscription, club subscription for all the workers, or through having copies in the church library. Their consistent use will provide any worker with a great deal of practical training for his work.

There should be books for workers in the church library. Some of these may deal with Christian education method. Others should provide background help in content, such as commentaries, atlas, books on the Bible, church history, worship resources. Providing such resources is only the first step. Workers need to be encouraged to use them.

A specific book, chapter, or article may be recommended as giving help on a problem. Books may be recommended in workers' meetings. A teacher may be asked to review a new book in such a meeting. Supplemental books may be given to teachers in addition to the lesson materials. Instruction may be given in the value and use of Bible commentaries and other helps.

4. *Observation-demonstration.* It is hard for most persons to translate oral or printed suggestions into practice. To see someone else do it is a great help in learning new and better methods. Interpretation of what is done should accompany observation, so that the learner may understand the *why* as well as see the *how*.

Opportunities for observation may be provided through (1) serving as assistant to an experienced worker, (2) visiting a good class or department within the church, (3) visiting another church school, (4) demonstration or laboratory work in connection with a training class, such as is provided by most summer schools.

Great benefit may be derived through having selected workers visit another church school where they may observe good practice. Such visits need to be carefully planned with the workers in the church to be visited to make sure that the visit will be fruitful. Prospective visitors should be prepared in advance so that they will know what to observe, and how to profit from it. Each visitor should attend a single department and class throughout the visit, and not just "look in on" what is going on throughout the church school.

Films and filmstrips which visualize good practice provide a means of demonstration, but this is not so effective as seeing good work at first hand.

5. *Guided Practice.* It has often been said that we learn

by doing, but this is true only if help is available to improve the first halting efforts and to correct mistakes. One value of a plan for assistant teachers is that they may be apprentices to experienced workers so that good practice can be learned under guidance. The vacation church school is especially useful in providing this kind of training.

The "workshop" is a good method for helping workers acquire new techniques. The students in the workshop not only hear explanations and see demonstrations, but actually practice the technique to be learned. This method may be used for teaching many kinds of skills, such as: lesson planning, story telling, map making, dramatization, group discussion, use of audio-visuals, creative projects of various types.

6. *Group Conferences.* Workers may learn a great deal through sharing with others in discussion and planning. Committee assignments and group meetings are a means of improving the work of the church school and helping workers to have a sense of responsibility and participation. Group conferences are not only more economical in time for the training leader than individual conferences, but also have other advantages. Workers will learn from each other as well as from the leader. The more reluctant ones will be carried along by those who are more enthusiastic. Resistance to new ways of doing things may be overcome by the testimony of those who are already using them. Training is thus not one-way communication from a leader to a group, but results from inter-actions within the group. Experienced workers will help the less experienced, and this is the more effective because all are "in the same boat." There are many types of group conferences—local church, denominational institutes and conventions, inter-denom-

inational meetings. The next section will deal in detail with the local church group conference.

7. *Leadership Classes.* The approaches to training listed above are informal, but nevertheless important and effective. Much of the training which workers receive comes to them through these informal means. The leadership training class is a more formal and systematic method. This will be treated in a subsequent section.

THE WORKERS' CONFERENCE

The term *workers' conference* is used to include all meetings of the church school staff which are held for the dual purpose of improving the work and training the workers. It is distinguished on the one hand from committees which have a definite job assigned them, and on the other hand from training classes, though it partakes of the nature of both. It provides an opportunity for workers to share in advancing the welfare of the church school and to gain inspiration and guidance for their own tasks. As the name implies, it is the workers' own and should be kept on a democratic basis, not used by the officers as an instrument solely for accomplishing their purpose.

1. *Types.* Workers' conferences are of two types: general and departmental. The general workers' conference should include all the officers, teachers, and other workers in Christian education, including the youth groups, vacation and weekday church schools, as well as the Sunday school. The departmental workers' conference should include all the workers in a given department, but the general officers may also be invited.

2. *Purposes.* Workers' conferences have four major purposes: (1) *Fellowship.* Workers need to develop a spirit of fellowship, a sense of togetherness in a mutual cause, of

support of one another. This comes best from worshiping and working together, but may be enhanced by having a supper together, a closing social period with refreshments, a community sing, and by introducing new workers to the whole group. It helps to give confidence to new workers to be drawn as soon as possible into such a fellowship group. (2) *Worship*. Workers should pray together. In a period devoted to worship they may confess their common dependence on God, ask for his guidance and blessing, and re-commit themselves to his service. If Christian education is to be centered in God, devotion to him must have an important place in the consciousness of workers. (3) *Business*. Matters of business are properly the responsibility of the committee on Christian education, not the workers' conference. Nevertheless, there are announcements to be made and instructions to be given, policies to be interpreted, and from time to time decisions to be made on matters which affect all the workers. A minimum time should be assigned to necessary business, and strictly adhered to. (4) *Education*. This will usually occupy the major part of the program. It may deal with any and all matters which will lead to improvement of the program and better preparation of the workers. Actually, the business and educational functions are often combined, because considerations of policy such as the place of missions in Christian education is an educative experience, while the recommendation of a plan resulting from this discussion is a business matter.

3. *Meetings*. Most churches find it desirable to hold general workers' conferences monthly. Some larger churches put more emphasis on departmental conferences and have only quarterly general meetings. Monthly departmental meetings are usually necessary. Evening meet-

ings are usual for general conferences, though some churches find it practical to meet early Sunday afternoon after a lunch at the church. Two hours is usually the maximum length, and time schedules should be strictly observed. Departmental meetings may be held at any time that is best for the workers involved. Mothers often find it convenient to attend while their children are in school, and some department staffs have found it possible to hold short meetings on Sunday morning outside the church school and church hours.

In order to avoid holding too many meetings, some churches combine general and departmental meetings in a single session. They may bring all workers together for the fellowship, worship, and business features, and substitute the departmental meetings for the educational feature. This plan is practical, but it should be recognized that it rarely allows enough time for the departments to do their work.

4. *Program.* The business and educational features of the workers' conference will normally grow out of the needs of the church school and its workers. The program should always be practical and relevant. Workers may have a share in deciding what the program is to be, through making suggestions, working on planning committees, sharing in presentation and discussion. Audio-visuals may be used whenever they are pertinent to the topic under discussion. Speakers from outside the church may be used, but only when a need has emerged to which they may make a contribution. The conference nature of these meetings should be maintained as much as possible, with the workers themselves sharing and not just listening.

The church school superintendent or the chairman of the committee on Christian education is normally the general chairman, though he need not preside throughout the session. The superintendent will usually conduct the business part of the meeting, but others may be in charge of fellowship periods, worship, and the educational period. If supper or refreshments are to be served, workers may take turns in helping with this, provided none of them have to be absent from any part of the program. Young people or other interested persons can be enlisted to help.

Department workers' conferences will be under the direction of the department principal, and may give more attention to the on-going work of the department than is possible in general conferences. Even though the staff is small, with only two or three teachers in each department, these few need to have informal meetings for planning together. One of the most useful things a department staff can do is to make a monthly preview of the lessons for the ensuing month. This is most practical when a departmental graded type of curriculum is in use, but may also be done with closely graded lessons.

This last suggestion is so important in the training of workers that further comment is desirable. Such previews give teachers the motivation to make long-range preparation. They enable teachers to be mutually helpful to each other in planning sessions. They give experience in lesson planning. They help to clear up problems in connection with the biblical and other material to be taught. They enable the principal to suggest helpful resources, and to work out ways of relating the department worship to class teaching. They offer opportunity for planning home activities. They make possible planning joint projects for the whole department. They may be in the nature of workshops for learning new methods. In short, such planning sessions may be the most important element in the training of workers. Once the teachers find the meetings practically helpful, there will be no problem in getting them to attend.

Programs for workers' conferences must be home-made if they are to be useful. Ready-made programs may be suggestive of what might be done locally, but usually need to be adapted for local use. The list of topics which follows is intended merely to illustrate what some churches have found profitable.

What Is Our Responsibility for Home Cooperation?
Buzz sessions in groups of 5 to suggest answers; two role plays to show how a home visit should be made.

What Should Be the Aim and Outcome of Our Teaching?
Presentation by a speaker, followed by discussion, and examination of aims as printed in the curriculum materials.

What Shall We Teach Concerning the Meaning of Easter?
This program was intended to help teachers clarify their own thinking. A New Testament scholar made the interpretation of the resurrection stories, followed by discussion.

Best Way to Prepare a Lesson
Pastor presented the steps in preparing to teach, using Lobingier, *If Teaching Is Your Job*, chapter 2. Followed by department meetings in each of which a teacher presented his plan for the next session, as an illustration for discussion.

How to Use Visual Aids
Filmstrip: *"The Use of Visual Method in the Church."* Followed by display of equipment and material in the church library, and practice in use of equipment.

How to Get the Most out of the Church Library
Church librarian explained use of the library and dis-

played books and pictures available to help teachers, also how to get additional material; minister demonstrated use of commentaries and bible dictionary.

Interest-getting Methods of Teaching
An outside leader explained and demonstrated some simple ways in which pupils may be involved in activity; followed by teachers telling about some methods they had found helpful.

How Do We Rate as a Church School?
Report of a committee appointed to make an evaluation; discussion of steps which might be taken to improve.

Why We Keep Records
Church school secretary, by means of charts and graphs, showed the record of attendance and enrollment through the year; emphasis on accurate record-keeping and follow-up.

The Significance of the Church in Our Teaching
Opening conference for the year in which the church is the curriculum emphasis. Presentation by the pastor, followed by departmental meetings for study of how the emphasis applies in each department.

The following schedule is suggested for an evening meeting of the general workers' conference:

6:15 Supper, followed by introductions and fellowship songs
7:00 Worship
7:15 Announcements and business
7:30 Presentation of educational topic, followed by discussion
8:30 Adjournment

If departmental conferences are to be held, these might begin at 8:00 and adjourn at 9:00 or 9:30. If supper is not included, the same schedule could be followed, opening at 7:30 and closing at 9:30 or 9:45.

5. *Attendance.* To serve its purpose, a workers' conference must be attended by all workers unless absence is unavoidable. The best attendance builder is an interesting, helpful program. Duties of workers should clearly include attendance at conferences. Regular monthly dates should be established in the church calendar. Reminders should be sent to each worker. Department principals may be expected to promote the attendance of their staffs. Sitters may be provided by the church for children of parents who could otherwise not attend. As a morale builder, there might be a roll-call at each meeting with department principals giving the reason for absence of those who do not respond.

6. *The Meeting Room.* The physical setting for the workers' conference is important to its success. The lighting should be ample, but subdued. Floor lamps and table lamps are better than glaring overhead lights. The seating arrangement should suggest participation. A circle pattern which enables everyone to see everyone else is better than rows of chairs. It is better for the chairman to be seated in this circle than to have a prominent place at the head of the room. If materials are to be displayed and used, or workshop activities engaged in, the members may be seated around a hollow square of tables. Comfortable chairs help people to feel at ease.

7. *For Further Help.* The filmstrip *Together We Grow,* in the Church School Administration Audio-visual Kit, is helpful toward understanding the nature, purpose, and method of the workers' conference. It might well be used

in one of the conference meetings to show all the workers how such meetings may be made more useful, and their responsibility in them. The 64-page manual *The Workers' Conference* by Verdia Burke, published by the Bethany Press, St. Louis, thoroughly covers every phase of the subject.

8. *Workers' Retreats.* A special type of workers' conference is the weekend retreat. This may be held at any time, but is most appropriate near the opening of the church school year. It may be held at a conference site, hotel, or other place which is remote enough to give people a sense of freedom from the daily round, and which provides facilities for the group to live and work together. It may be held from Friday evening through Saturday afternoon, or even Sunday afternoon if church school is not in session.

The retreat provides opportunity for worship, fellowship, and study, at a leisurely pace which is not possible in single-session meetings. The program should seek to deepen the devotional life, enrich the worker's own knowledge and understanding of the Christian faith, interpret and evaluate the church's work in Christian education, and consider the program and problems of the new year. It will provide opportunity for whole-group sessions as well as department and other small group conferences. It is especially useful in integrating new workers into the staff and instructing them in their work.

A retreat must be carefully planned and vigorously promoted. Outside resource leaders may be used, but the program should be relevant to the church's own needs, and get participation by as many of the workers as possible. Workers who are parents may need some help in providing for the care of children while they are away. A way of meeting this problem, as well as of adding other values to the retreat, is to make provision for whole families to attend, with a program for children which parallels the work sessions.

TRAINING CLASSES AND SCHOOLS

Courses for prospective teachers as well as teachers in service provide more intensive training than the more informal methods thus far discussed. Such courses usually have from five to ten sessions, and require at least an equal amount of time to be spent in preparation. Students are expected to study text-books and other reading material, and to engage in projects related to the courses.

Denominational boards provide curricula for workers' training, including suggested courses, recommended text-books, and in some cases teaching guides. Students are awarded credits for courses completed under standard conditions. Information concerning such curricula, conditions for credit, and procedure in enrolling a class will be sent on request. These denominational curricula are based on a program of training developed cooperatively by their representatives through the Division of Christian Education of the National Council of Churches.

1. *Where Training Is Offered.* Training courses may be taken in local church classes, community training schools, and in summer schools of Christian education.

(1) Local church classes may be conducted for two types of students: (a) Prospective workers, young people, and others who are willing to take such training in preparation for service. Such courses may well be a part of the regular curriculum, with classes meeting on Sunday morning. (b) Workers already in service who are interested in improving themselves and their work. Classes for these

will of necessity meet outside the church school hour, usually on a weeknight. They may include prospective workers as well as workers already in service. Local church classes have the advantage of being able to relate training to the program and problems of the church school in which the students are serving or preparing to serve.

(2) Community training schools are conducted by the churches of a community in cooperation. They usually provide a number of courses from which a choice may be made. Compared with local church classes, they have such advantages as these: (a) they can provide more specialized courses; (b) they can usually have the services of a more expert faculty; (c) it is mutually helpful for workers from different churches to get acquainted and work together. Since community schools usually require a registration fee, it is proper for local churches to pay this fee for all their own workers who attend.

(3) Summer schools are conducted by many denominations, and some are inter-denominational in character. Denominational schools usually provide for study and experience in the use of the denominational curriculum for the church school. Increasingly this is done by means of a "laboratory" school, in which students may observe the work of competent teachers and relate their study and discussion to this observation. Experience has proved that such a combination of practice, observation, and study is the most effective means of training. It is a wise plan for local churches to select one or more of their most promising workers and send them to a summer school, with expenses paid in whole or in part. A few key workers with this intensive training may be the means of transforming the whole church school.

2. *Types of Courses.* Training courses may be of two

general types, the one serving the worker's own need for better understanding of the faith, and the other helping him in doing his job.

(1) While workers have usually had the benefit of Christian education throughout their childhood and youth, most of them need further education in Bible, theology, church history, and other fields of Christian knowledge. Such courses should have a large place in the training curriculum.

(2) The second type of training course is aimed at helping the worker to learn the methods of effective teaching, or whatever skills his job requires. This includes understanding of pupils and how they learn, the nature of Christian education, the organization and administration of the church school, how to conduct worship, techniques of teaching, and effective methods of working with individuals and groups.

(3) The purposes of these two types of courses merge into one another. The worker who gets a better understanding of the faith will thereby be enabled to do his work with greater confidence and effectiveness; conversely, practice can have little meaning apart from purpose and content. Some workers may be heard to say that they do not take training courses because they do not find them practical. This is a serious indictment, for the very purpose of training is to assure better practice. Nevertheless, those responsible for training should never be satisfied unless workers have gained a better understanding of and deeper insight into the faith which they are teaching as well as the methods by which it may be communicated.

3. *Methods of Teaching.* Training is never something that a teacher does *to* others. The students must be involved in their own training if they are to profit by it.

Such involvement is best accomplished by relating training as closely as possible to practice. People do not become skillful simply by reading books or listening to lectures, though these may be very effective when seen in relation to practice. This is why laboratory school experience is so effective. It is an argument in favor of training workers in service, after they have first been confronted by the problems on which they need help. A local church training class may well include an opportunity for the students to observe in classes and departments of the church school in relation to class study.

Audio-visuals are useful in relating training to practice because they help students to visualize actual teaching situations. The training teacher should be familiar with the better subjects which have been produced for the training of workers and make generous use of them.

4. *Who shall teach the training class?* The answer to this question is simple: The one best qualified by personality, education, and experience. This will vary with different courses. The minister is best qualified to teach some of the courses. Experienced lay workers may be best fitted to handle some of the more specialized subjects. The need for constant renewal and improvement in the staff justifies relieving the person most capable of conducting training classes from other duties. In some cases it may be necessary to bring someone from outside the local church to conduct a training class.

It is not necessary in every case to have a highly qualified teacher for the training class. A good deal can be accomplished by a group through cooperatively studying together. Usually in such a group there is someone who can serve as leader in guiding their study, even though he does not feel competent to take the more formal role of teacher.

Teachers of training classes may themselves get needed preparation through attendance at a community training school or summer school.

5. *Motivation.* "How can we interest our workers in taking training?" This question comes up again and again. We may as well face the hard fact. There is no way of "making" workers do what they do not want to do. There are no sure-fire tricks which will solve this problem.

(1) Basically, the problem goes back to the attitudes that workers have toward their work. If they have enlisted in the church school staff because of deep conviction that this is the way they can best express their Christian commitment, if they humbly recognize that they are not yet the best workmen they could be, they will be interested in making the necessary effort to improve themselves in their work. There must be a sense of need before we may expect effort. This is basic to all good teaching.

(2) There must be the assurance, born of experience, that participation in training will be helpful. The training program should be such that workers participating in it will consider their time and effort well repaid.

(3) The promise of opportunity for training, and the expectation that he will participate in it, needs to be a part of the understanding with a worker when he is appointed to service.

(4) Credits may judiciously be used to give workers a goal, and a sense of achievement in training. Like all awards, the training credit must never be the reason for taking courses, but only the symbol of achievement. One church used this method of motivation by displaying an honor roll which bore the names of all the members of the church school staff, followed by an indication of the training courses that each had completed.

(5) To bring these factors to bear on the training problem, there will need to be wise and friendly promotion of the training enterprises. Personal invitations to workers to enroll in the community school or a local class are a far more effective method than general announcements.

13 ROOMS AND EQUIPMENT

Program and workers are more important than rooms and equipment. There are many churches in which good Christian education is carried on with inadequate space and meager equipment. But other things being equal, better work can be done when adequate facilities are available. Even the best workman needs a workshop and good tools with which to work.

A good building and proper equipment do not guarantee a good program, but they do encourage and facilitate effective work. On the other hand, if rooms are inadequate in number and size, and if there is not adequate equipment, the program will be limited by these conditions. While comparatively few churches can have all that a good program requires, much can be done to make the most of what is available through the use of imagination and ingenuity in organization and administration, and through judicious efforts for improvement.

Some churches are in the fortunate situation of being able to improve their facilities through new building, remodeling, or refurnishing. For them the question is: What is ideal? How can we realize the ideal? Others must carry on with what they have. For them the question is: How can we make the most of existing resources? How can we idealize the real?

PLANNING TO BUILD

The scope of this book does not allow a full treatment of matters related to building for Christian education. Readers who are confronting this opportunity are advised to get the book *Building and Equipping for Christian Education* by C. Harry Atkinson, published by the National Council of Churches, and to correspond with their denominational board of Christian education for advice and help. However, since many churches are expanding and improving their physical facilities, a few suggestions are in order here to guide the church school workers in such churches.

A church building is good to the extent that it serves the needs of the congregation. A building can be planned only in light of the program which it is to serve. An architect can make a plan after he knows what is needed properly to serve the program; he should not be expected to tell the church what it needs.

A church building must serve many purposes—worship, preaching, fellowship, recreation, as well as Christian education. A first step in planning is to have competent committees, representing each of these interests, make the necessary studies on the basis of which recommendations can be made. These separate recommendations need then to be brought together into a comprehensive whole. Compromises will no doubt be necessary, because it is rarely possible to get everything that everybody wants, but adjustments can best be made after the total needs have been outlined.

1. *Planning for Christian Education.* The committee on Christian education is the proper group to study the needs and make the recommendations for Christian education. This committee should seek the best available guidance in making its studies. Unless the planning is done very carefully, there will be tragic mistakes, and such mistakes cannot be corrected after they have been embodied in brick and stone. Following are some of the major questions which need to be answered:

(1) For how many pupils do we need to provide? How will they be distributed through the several departments? Present enrollment is only one part of the answer. What of the future? What predictions can we make for the next 25 or 50 years? If there are prospects for a large future increase, the building may need to be so planned as to allow the addition of new units in the future.

(2) How should the church school be organized? How many departments should we have? Shall we follow the 2-year or the 3-year department plan? How many classes in each department? What size classes shall we have? Do we need to have the whole church school at the same hour, or can we make multiple use of rooms by having two or more sessions? Can one chapel or department room be used by two or more departments, or do we need to have a separate worship room for each department? Can older groups use the church sanctuary for department worship?

(3) What type of program do we want? How much space does this require for each pupil? A program in which there is a good deal of pupil activity requires more space than one in which each pupil occupies a fixed position throughout the session. It is a general rule that the younger

the child the more space he needs. Standardized figures on required classroom space vary all the way from 25 to 35 square feet per pupil for nursery and kindergarten to 8 to 10 for adults.

Shall we have a unified program, including worship, in primary and junior classes, as is customary for nursery and kindergarten? If so, no meeting room for department worship is needed. But classrooms need to be larger to allow for additional activities, and under this plan classes are usually also larger.

In which rooms will projected audio-visual aids be used? This requires provision for proper darkening, and electrical outlets which are not on the same circuit with the room lights. In chapels and auditoriums a conduit should be built into the floor or ceiling to carry the sound connection from projector to speaker, and it is desirable to have a projection booth outside the room.

(4) Some of these problems require answers that are difficult to give. They require decisions on educational policy. They require projection of plans into the future when no one knows what future trends may be. But it is better to face them courageously and make the best decisions possible than to run the risk of having a new building which is out of date before it is completed. It is an excellent tonic for the educational program to have a responsible group facing such vital questions of policy.

Some guidance can be had from visiting other churches which have good new buildings. This must be done with great care, so that their mistakes will not be copied along with their good qualities.

It is a good plan to enlist the services of a specialist in Christian education to help the local workers in thinking through these problems. This will help to assure that the best current trends are taken into account. A small investment in such service may help to avoid unfortunate and costly mistakes, and will be useful in convincing the church of the needs in Christian education which the new building should meet.

2. *Some Guiding Principles.* These studies should lead to conclusions concerning number of rooms required, type and size of rooms, desirable furnishings. The following considerations should be helpful in spelling out the requirements in greater detail:

(1) With regard to rooms, the youngest children should have the most favorable location, on the first floor. Basement rooms should be avoided, and in any case, rooms should not be more than three feet below surface level. In view of changing trends in size of classrooms, the building should be so constructed that partitions between rooms can be changed so as to provide larger or smaller rooms when this becomes desirable. Partitions should be sound proof. Rooms should be rectangular, with ample unbroken wall space. Each room should be accessible from a corridor. Folding partitions to allow changing a larger room into two or more smaller ones should be used only if absolutely necessary. They are expensive and not usually practical. Storage cupboards should be provided in each room, and more extensive storage space in other parts of the building. Lavatories should be accessible and ample. A place should be provided for hanging coats and hats, either in the classroom or near it. A room for the administrative office is very desirable.

(2) Interior decoration and furnishings are properly included in the budget for a new building. Recommendations for desirable equipment will follow in the next section. Unfortunately, in many cases financial resources are

exhausted before this point is reached. Under these conditions, we advise the church school officers: (a) Do not allow your church school rooms to become a museum for the cast-off furnishings from the old church. Accept only such items as are really usable. (b) If unsuitable equipment must be used temporarily, such as tables and chairs of improper size, make sure that they will be replaced as soon as possible. (c) In buying new equipment, get only that which is substantial and proper for long-time use. It is better to move more slowly in buying good equipment as financial resources make this possible than to get cheap merchandise which needs to be replaced in a year or two and is never satisfactory.

(3) It is painfully evident that the well equipped church school building requires a large investment. Some will argue that, considering the comparatively few hours per week that such a building is used, this cost is greater than most churches can or should bear. We must answer that the importance of good facilities for effective Christian education is so great that it cannot be measured in terms of dollars and cents. However, if we cannot get all we need—and few churches can—some compromises will need to be made. These adjustments should be, not in the direction of lowering the standards of good rooms and equipment, but of well-planned multiple use. In most churches it is not necessary to carry out all Sunday school activities in the limited time of one hour. Schedules can be devised which permit the use of some rooms by two or more groups of approximately the same age. If the entire school can be divided vertically into two equal halves, meeting at two different hours, the available facilities will serve twice as many people. Thus an imaginative use of time may compensate for lack of space.

USING WHAT YOU HAVE

The more usual problem confronted by administrative officers is not that of planning a new building, but that of making the best use of what already exists. Within the limits of existing buildings, creative imagination and hard work can often result in remarkable improvement.

1. *Location of Departments and Classes.* A study of available space, with a view to using every room and alcove to the best advantage, may result in reassignments of space for more effective use. Room assignments should always be in the control of the church school officers. No group has a proprietary right to any given space. In carrying out this principle, a problem may be encountered with adult groups who by tradition have occupied rooms which are more needed by others. With tactful handling, the adults of the church should be willing to concede that it is the younger children who have the greatest need for good meeting places.

What has been said earlier about the multiple use of rooms is pertinent to this problem of making the most effective use of existing space and equipment.

(1) *The One-room Church.* In what has been said thus far we have assumed that there are several rooms available for the church school. We are not unmindful of the fact that some churches have only one room which must serve all purposes, or one main room with only one or two small additional rooms. It can be argued that where this condition has been allowed to exist through the years there can be no great sense of the importance of Christian education. Certainly no new buildings should be erected which do not make some provision for separate rooms for the church school. But what advice can be given to the officers of church schools who must work under this limitation?

(a) It cannot be denied that effective Christian education may be done even under these conditions. Usually such churches have other assets which work in their favor. Membership is small, and there is a closer inter-relationship between the young and older persons. Church school and church can more easily be unified. The minister can have a larger place in church school leadership.

(b) The Christian education program in such a church needs to be adapted to the existing condition. Worship services will need to be more in the nature of family worship than graded departmental services. Teaching method needs to be adapted to require less pupil activity than is possible in separate classrooms. Rather than lamenting their inability to do all that is desirable for a varied and rich program, workers need to use to the best advantage those things which can be done under their conditions.

(c) Creative imagination will suggest ways of using the single room to best advantage. Classes may be distributed in the room with a view to maximum separation. Corners or alcoves may be screened for a measure of privacy. Movable chairs may be placed in areas not occupied by pews. Lap boards may be provided for older pupils, and younger children may use the seats of pews for work space by kneeling in front of them. In some cases it may be possible to provide separate worship for a small group of young children in a screened corner or alcove.

(2) *The Two-room Church.* There are many other churches which, while not limited to one room, still fall far short of having adequate space for the church school. They may have one large room in addition to the church sanctuary, and perhaps a few smaller rooms. This large room is used for many purposes, such as dining room, general meeting room, recreation room, as well as the

work of the church school. It cannot be divided into smaller rooms for the church school. Under these conditions, the following might be done:

(a) Give the younger children the advantage in assigning the separate rooms.

(b) Use the sanctuary for adults and older boys and girls.

(c) Provide screening of some kind for classes which meet in the large room. This may be done by means of curtains or movable screens. Curtains may be hung on wires or pipes, or mounted on rollers. In case of a room with a high ceiling, it is practical to hinge the pipes or rods carrying the curtains at the wall so that by a pulley arrangement they may be pulled up at the free end and be out of the way when not in use. Screen surfaces may serve as chalkboards and mounting boards. Curtains and screens have no value in reducing disturbing noises, but they do give classes a sense of privacy and cosiness. Unfortunately, neither of these devices can be used satisfactorily in the sanctuary because one cannot mount curtains without an unsightly maze of wires or pipes, and there is usually no convenient place to put such large screens when not in use.

2. *Improving Equipment.* Additions to educational equipment can be made a little at a time. The annual budget should carry an item for this so that the most pressing needs may be met from year to year. In purchasing new equipment, good quality and permanence are more important than immediate price. Catalogs of firms which supply school and church furniture, such as the American Seating Company of New York and Chicago, should be consulted for suggestions of desirable equipment and specifications for proper sizes of tables and chairs for pupils of different ages.

The particular items of equipment which are needed depend to some extent on the program to be served, but the following will be commonly used:

(1) *Coat Rooms or Racks.* Pupils and teachers should be encouraged to remove coats and hats on arrival. For older pupils it is desirable to have a coatroom conveniently located or a rack outside the classrooms. Similar provision should be made in the classroom for young children.

(2) *Worship Rooms.* Rooms used for worship should be arranged with great care so as to provide the proper atmosphere. The church sanctuary provides the pattern, and in many cases the sanctuary should be used, especially for whole-school services or for older departments, rather than some other room which is poorly adapted. Ideally, the room should be twice as long as it is wide. It should have a chancel arrangement at one end, equipped with a worship center, pulpit and lectern, chairs for leaders and small tables for offering plates and flower vases. Pews or chairs of proper height should be arranged in straight rows facing the chancel, and with a center aisle if possible. A piano or organ should be so placed as to make it possible for the musician to see the leader and follow his directions. A storage cabinet for hymnals and other materials is desirable. If audio-visuals are to be used, there should be a concealed screen which can be drawn into place when needed, opaque curtains, and a table or booth for projectors.

(3) *Classrooms* need to be equipped with substantial chairs of proper size for pupils and teacher, and some type of work space. For the latter, tables are commonly used in church school rooms. The best style table is rectangular, 24 inches to 30 inches by 48 inches to 60 inches, thus making it possible to arrange the several units in various

formations to suit the activity of the class. For younger children, it is desirable to avoid tables with stretcher supports near the edges, so that there will be ample room for their knees. Drawers in classroom tables are not desirable. Natural wood finish is best. For older pupils, when classes are fairly large, chairs equipped with chair-desks or tablet arms are better than tables and chairs.

Other desirable equipment will include: bookshelves and browsing table, chalkboard and bulletin board, storage cabinet for teacher's and pupils' materials, picture rail, opaque shades, maps. Younger children will need painting easels, toys, and numerous other items appropriate to their activities.

(4) *Storage Closets.* Each teacher needs a space of his own for storage of materials and supplies between Sundays. General storage space is needed for audio-visual equipment, other equipment when not in use, books and supplies being preserved for use in subsequent years.

3. *Servicing.* A good janitor is an invaluable asset to Christian education. No matter how humble the building or how meager the equipment, they can at least be kept neat and clean. Good housekeeping for the church school is something in which every worker may take a hand, for no matter whose responsibility it is, we must in any event see to it that rooms and equipment are in proper condition when the time comes to use them. A dustcloth is a necessary item for every teacher.

Too many church schools present a dismal picture when it comes to cleanliness and orderliness. Who has not seen a piano piled high with old lesson materials, pews and chairs littered with papers from the previous session, storage cabinets cluttered with all kinds of "junk" from past quarters, unused pianos in odd places tempting early pupils to try their musical skill with discordant results (to avoid this, keep them locked), classrooms marred with the dejected aspect of broken chairs? This ought not to be, and need not be. How to dispose of discarded material and equipment is an art only second in importance to acquiring what is needed.

Every church needs a repair department to which equipment in need of servicing can be sent. As in the case of human disease, if symptoms are recognized early and treatment given promptly, this will prevent more serious consequences later.

Audio-visual equipment is especially in need of care and regular servicing. It is a good plan to make one person or a committee fully responsible for this. It is a job which high school boys can do.

Rooms should not only be clean and orderly, but also be as attractive as possible. Curtains and draperies, a good scrubbing now and then, an occasional coat of paint, a new shelf or bookcase, will do much to help make rooms livable and pleasant. Here is one place where parents can go into action in the interest of the church school.

4. *Remodeling.* It is sometimes possible to make an inadequate building serve the needs of the church school better by some judicious alterations. A major job of remodeling requires some of the same procedures as planning for a new building, but simple alterations may be carried out under the direction of the church school officers, while "business as usual" is going on. This may include reconditioning an unused basement area; partitioning a large room to make several smaller ones, or changing two small rooms into one larger one; installing acoustical ceiling tile or floor covering; installing needed lavatories; providing electrical outlets; building bookcases, storage

cabinets, coat racks. Much of this kind of work may be done by voluntary labor. Some items of furniture and play equipment may also be home-made, but the results are rarely as good as factory-made equipment.

5. *Utilization.* Equipment serves no good purpose unless workers make use of it. Chalkboards, maps, audio-visual equipment, reference books, bulletin boards, are available in some churches but rarely used. The probable reason is that teachers have not learned how helpful such aids can be in teaching. They need training in good utilization, and this training could be an interesting feature in the workers' conference program.

Chalkboards may go unused because it seems to be impossible to keep them supplied with crayon and eraser. Encourage each teacher to carry his own with his other teaching materials. This will also avoid misuse of the board by pupils before and after class sessions.

14 RECORDS, ATTENDANCE AND ENROLLMENT, TIME SCHEDULES, FINANCES

This final chapter will deal with a number of separate problems, which are more or less related.

CHURCH SCHOOL RECORDS

Two words describe the purpose of church school records: *guidance* and *measurement*. Records serve as guidance to the workers by providing information on the constituency to be served: the numbers in each grade for which organization, equipment, and leadership must be provided; the home background, previous training, and present needs of each pupil. They serve as measurement by showing how well the constituency is being reached and held, where the points of strength and weakness are, and how well the church school is doing its job.

The permanent record will show the history of the

church school through the years. This will include such material as: (1) A card or sheet for each pupil, showing his Christian education progress from the time he enrolls. This will give data on his residence, date of birth, date of enrollment, date baptized, date joining the church, and a cumulative record of his performance each year, such as membership in different agencies of the church school, attendance, work completed and other achievements, date of withdrawal if this should occur, and reason for same. (2) A record of each agency, giving statistics of enrollment and attendance for each session and summaries for each year, officers, and so on.

In addition to the data for the permanent record, each agency, class, and group will record other items which are immediately useful but not carried into the permanent record. A teacher may record personal items about each pupil, such as family background, interests, class response and conduct, work completed, evidences of Christian growth. A department will have a list of its staff, classes, pupils; records of attendance; a file of worship services and other programs. The church school or any of its agencies should have a list of prospective members.

1. *Unity of Record System.* If, as has been maintained, the entire educational program should be a unified whole, the record system should maintain this essential unity. The permanent record of each pupil should cover his performance in all the agencies—Sunday school, youth groups, vacation church school, and others. Data on enrollment, attendance, and scope of the church's program should include all the agencies. Within this unified system, each agency will have its own records, from which some of the data will be passed on for the unified record while other items will be only for its own use. The general secretary

will serve the whole church school, while the secretary for each agency will be an assistant to him with responsibility for his own agency. A large Sunday school needs departmental secretaries to assist the secretary of the school.

2. *Definition of Terms.* In order that records may be intelligible and useful, it is desirable that there be agreement on the meaning of certain terms. The following were suggested by the International Council of Religious Education:

(1) *Registration* signifies the initial enrollment of a pupil in the church school, and his re-enrollment in any of its agencies at the beginning of the year.

(2) *Enrollment* includes all pupils who are on the list in any one year. It is an increasing number as the year progresses, and will be highest at the end of the year.

(3) *Attending membership* includes the total number on the active list. This number will vary from week to week. It is usually less than the enrollment because it excludes those who withdraw or become inactive in the course of the year.

(4) *Attendance* includes all who are present for any given session. *Average attendance* is determined by totaling the attendance for all the sessions for which the average is sought and dividing this number by the number of sessions.

(5) *Percentage of attendance* is arrived at by dividing the attendance by the attending membership for any given session, or the averages of these for any desired period of time.

(6) *Tardiness* means arrival after the hour and minute established for the opening of the session.

(7) *Absence* means non-attendance for any reason whatsoever.

251

3. *When should a pupil be enrolled?* When anyone seriously presents himself (or in the case of young children, is brought by his parents) to any agency of the church school with the intention of becoming a member he should be accepted for enrollment. There is no need for a probationary period, except in cases when he or his family signify that he has not yet decided to become a member. Such a person may be regarded as a visitor until the decision is reached.

New pupils should be cordially welcomed, assigned to the proper department and class, and introduced to the leaders and other pupils. A visit to the home should be made as soon as possible to get necessary data for the permanent record, and to interpret the curriculum and the work of the church school to the pupil and his family. This is the time to impress the importance of regular attendance and serious work.

In case of church families, a child should be enrolled in the nursery roll on the day he is born. When he arrives at the earliest age for which church school activities are provided, his parents should be invited to enroll him in the active attending membership.

4. *When should a pupil be withdrawn?* Permanent withdrawal should be recorded as soon as it is clear that a pupil will no longer attend, which may be because of removal from the community, change to another church, death, or a responsible statement by him or his parents that he wishes to terminate his connection. The last named cause will not be accepted until everything possible has been done to revive his interest.

Temporary withdrawals are provided for pupils who are inactive over a period of time. This is a device for keeping the attending membership really active. Such persons are placed on an inactive list, with the expectation that they will return and again be added to the attending membership. Three consecutive absences may be established as a cause for temporary withdrawal. This allows sufficient time for follow-up to determine the cause of absence and to encourage return. The inactive list should be a constant challenge to teachers and officers to evangelistic effort with pupils and their families.

5. *What should be recorded?* The basic unit for record making is the class or other small group. Teachers and group leaders are important adjuncts to the secretarial staff. The effectiveness and value of the entire record system depends on their accuracy and diligence. From the class records certain basic data will be passed on to become a part of the general record.

Each class and group will have a record book or individual record card for each member. A book is better than individual cards, because a card is too easily thrown out or otherwise lost. This book will have a list of members, both active and inactive, with information including address, telephone, father's name and occupation, birthday, age, and school grade.

In spaces provided for each session, the leader will mark attendance, tardies, new pupils enrolled and those re-instated from the inactive list, temporary and permanent withdrawals. A summary line will indicate enrollment, attending membership, number inactive, number and percent present. These facts are essential for the record book. In addition, the leader should have a supplemental record of such other facts about each pupil as were suggested above. Since the record book will be returned to the secretary's office after each session, the leader should have a duplicate list for use during the week.

6. *What ought the attendance to be?* The best index of the health of a church school is the percentage of average attendance. Public school attendance runs well above 90 percent. Should church schools do as well? Perhaps, but the fact is that they do not. One reason for the difference is that church schools enroll very young children and adults, and in both cases the attendance is likely to be more sporadic than with school age children. But even in the school grades, Sunday schools rarely attain 90 percent attendance. Vacation church schools and weekday church schools do much better. Sunday attendance is not taken as seriously as weekday attendance, and it requires constant effort to help parents realize the importance of continuity if Christian education is to be effective.

One of our correspondents states that his Sunday school averages 300 present out of a total of 380. This is just under 80 percent, which is good when compared with Sunday schools generally. When percentage of attendance is figured on the basis of active (attending) membership, as suggested above, 75 percent to 85 percent attendance should not be an impossible ideal. When it is figured on the basis of total enrollment, it is rarely possible to go above 65 percent to 75 percent.

7. *Administration of Records.* Adequate and accurate records are so important that the best person available needs to be enlisted to serve as secretary. It may be a person who does not care to serve in other capacities, but whose training, experience, and interest make him eminently qualified for this job. In carrying out his duties he needs the help of the church school staff. The following plans will facilitate record taking:

(1) Keep the record system as simple as is consistent with its purpose. It can easily be so complex that record

taking becomes a major job of the teacher and interferes with his primary duties.

(2) Do not interrupt classes to distribute and collect record books. Have the teachers pick them up when they arrive and return them at the close of church school; or distribute them to classrooms before the session, and collect them after its close. The secretary's work with these record books does not need to be done during the church school hour.

(3) Do not make the marking of the record a first item in the class session. To do so may lead to disorder and failure to get a good start in the session. After a few sessions, teachers should know their pupils so well that the record can be marked immediately after the session, or at some point in the session when pupils are engaged in activity. Marking the record should not be left to pupils. The teacher needs to be confronted each session with his class list and the facts concerning each pupil.

(4) Have a registration day at the opening of each school year, so as to begin with an accurate list of pupils. Those enrolled in previous years who have not returned should be followed up immediately.

(5) In large Sunday schools, have a secretary for each department who acts as assistant to the general secretary. He may handle the distribution and collection of class books, and tabulate the summaries for the benefit of both the general secretary and the department principal.

8. *Utilization of Records.* The very fact of keeping accurate records is a good tonic for workers and pupils. However, records will not serve their purpose unless the conditions and facts they show are utilized by the church school staff. What do they show concerning trends in enrollment and attendance? Which departments and

classes show strength and which weakness? Where are the trouble spots about which something must be done? By means of graphs and charts, and judicious use of statistics, the secretary can be helpful in guiding the workers, as well as adding an interesting item to workers' meetings. The superintendent, in particular, should look for guidance to the secretary in locating and solving many of the problems of the church school. The following section will show how records may be useful as a basis for increasing attendance and enrollment.

9. *Record Systems.* The best system of records should normally be one which the church school workers themselves devise to meet their own needs. Unfortunately, this is usually not possible because of the complexity of the problem and the expense of duplicating record forms. It will therefore be necessary to use a published system and adapt it to local needs. It is suggested that the superintendent correspond with his denominational board of Christian education for advice on the best system to use.

INCREASING ATTENDANCE AND ENROLLMENT

Any church's total output in Christian education is determined by three factors: (1) the quality of its work, (2) the time available for Christian teaching, (3) the number of pupils served.[1] To increase any one of these without detriment to the others is to increase the product.

1. *Improving Attendance.* Our first concern is with those who are already enrolled. If they attend regularly, this will not only increase the number served in any given session, but also make the work with each person more effective. Good attendance is the result of systematic and

---

[1] This formula is proposed and fully developed in the book *How to Increase Your Sunday School* by Harry C. Munro. Bethany Press, 1926.

continuous effort. Contests and awards are not the answer. A good and interesting program is basic, but to this a judicious promotion of attendance must be added.

Parents need to be educated in the need for prompt and regular attendance. Too many of them do not realize how significant this is in maintaining pupil interest and achieving results. Personal interest in pupils, expressing itself in concern for absences and in encouragement of regular attendance, is necessary. Classes will learn to take pride in their own performances through the use of charts and diagrams showing their record from week to week. Attendance promotion is primarily the responsibility of teachers and group leaders, and any teacher who works at it systematically will be gratified with the results. Teachers may well be expected to report on reasons for absence before a pupil is temporarily withdrawn because of three absences.

(1). *The Post-confirmation Problem.* Most churches experience a falling-off of attendance soon after and even during the junior high school age. This seems to be a particularly vexing problem immediately after confirmation and joining the church. With some pupils this is a conscious transition from childhood to young adulthood, from Sunday school to attendance at church. Church attendance is a desirable outcome of Christian education, and we should be disappointed if this did not happen. But Christian education should not stop at that time. These pupils have only just reached the age when some of the more profound biblical and theological teaching can be done. They are undergoing new experiences in school and personal and social life to which Christian teaching needs to be related.

The problem arises in part from the fact that in many

churches the Sunday school is regarded as primarily for children. It will be solved in large measure by having a vigorous program which includes all ages, and particularly adults.

Another cause of the problem is the comparative weakness of the church school program in older departments. The solution for this is to put more effort on developing a strong program which is appropriate to the interests and abilities of youth. To this must be added the usual efforts of promoting enrollment and attendance.

It must be recognized also that Christian education may be given through other agencies than the Sunday school. If interest in the Sunday school has waned, the desired results can still be achieved through the youth fellowships and other activities. All these agencies are the church in action, and *where* young people receive their Christian teaching is not as important as that *somewhere* they do get their rightful heritage.

(2) *The Problem of Tardiness.* The time factor is affected when pupils and teachers are tardy. If this causes leaders to start their sessions late, so much the worse. Tardiness is a malady with which many church people are afflicted. It is an insult to the sacredness and importance of the church for people to regard it as of no significance to be on time. If Christian education can help to train a new generation of church members who have overcome this sin, it will achieve an important objective. But can the problem be solved?

While it may be too much to expect a complete solution, we believe that the following suggestions will get results:

Institute an educational campaign with the entire constituency on the importance of being on time. Get all workers to agree to come at least 15 minutes before opening. Provide interesting activities for pupils who come early to encourage them in this. Start all sessions on time, and consider everyone tardy who is not present at the minute of opening. It is a vicious practice to consider people on time if they come in during the first hymn. If there is an opening service of worship, admit persons only at stated points when their entrance will not be disturbing. Emphasize being on time with individual pupils. Make tardies a matter of record and let pupils know how they stand on this. If report cards are sent to the home, include tardies as an item. On the positive side, emphasize the importance of giving the church its full due.

(3) *Length of Sessions.* Time for Christian education can be increased by lengthening church school sessions. Although 60-minute sessions are traditional, there is no good reason why they should not run 75 or 90 minutes, and some churches have "expanded" sessions of two hours. When 60 minutes are divided between worship and class, there is not enough time for the kind of creative teaching that most good curricula assume. An unfortunate circumstance when there are two or more sessions of the Sunday school to accommodate large numbers in an inadequate building is that this usually limits the length of sessions to little more than an hour. This is particularly true when Sunday school parallels the church service. Even in such cases some churches find it feasible to start the Sunday school 15 minutes in advance of the opening of the church service.

Good teaching requires class periods of ample length. They should never be less than 30 minutes, and 40 to 60 minutes if possible. When time is limited, it is best to keep worship services short and not to sacrifice on class time.

Leaders of worship must guard against allowing their services to encroach on class time.

Just as important as the scheduled length of the session is the need for making the full amount of time available by starting promptly and not dismissing early. Superintendents should make particular effort to have all sessions begin on time, and when dismissal is from classes teachers should be expected to hold their classes until the signal for dismissal is given. If one class is dismissed early, it is hard for other teachers to keep their classes at work.

2. *Increasing Enrollment.* Many church schools are already overcrowded, and the problem of reaching additional people does not interest them. Others can well absorb more members. In any case, every church has an evangelistic responsibility for the large numbers who are not now receiving Christian education. Hence reaching new pupils must be a constant concern.

The first responsibility of every church school is to its own church constituency. As long as there are members of families who are not in the church school, effort needs to be made to enlist them. The second responsibility is to the Protestant people of the community who are not enrolled in other church schools. A community survey will reveal that there are many of these in most communities.

A good program which recommends itself through the members who are participating in it is a necessary basis for enlisting others. Pupils may be encouraged to invite their friends to come, and in many cases will do so even without being urged.

A systematic plan for membership cultivation may be instituted, using the lists of prospects already suggested. One denomination makes the assistant superintendent responsible for this. Such continuing effort is better than any high pressure campaign.

If transportation is a problem, bus service may be established, or a plan worked out for car pools. Some members of the church accept responsibility for conducting the church school; why should not others give their service in helping pupils to attend?[2]

The vacation church school presents an annual problem of promotion of enrollment. The Sunday school constituency provides a natural field for this. Promotion should be extended to all the homes of the parish. Also, since the vacation church school is usually regarded more as a community activity than a denominational enterprise, promotion may be freely extended to the whole community through newspapers, posters, postcards, house-to-house canvass, and many types of public announcement. In many cases the vacation church school will enlist boys and girls who are not in any Sunday school.

FINANCING THE CHURCH SCHOOL

The proper financial policy grows out of our understanding of the place of Christian education in the church. (1) The church school is the church at work, discharging its responsibility for Christian teaching. Hence its support should be provided in the annual budget of the church. (2) The pupils in the church school are to regard themselves as participants in the church fellowship. Hence their giving should be to the church and the causes which it supports.

---

[2] Most denominational boards are prepared to supply helpful material on membership enlistment. See for example, *The Membership Cultivation Manual*, Methodist Publishing House, Nashville, Tenn. and *How to Get More Members in Your Church School*, Board of Christian Education and Publication, Evangelical and Reformed Church, Philadelphia.

In many churches, however, this ideal has not been achieved. Church schools provide for their own support, through the offerings of the pupils. While this is not sound in principle, it represents an existing situation under which the workers must operate. Steps should be taken to remedy the condition, but several years may be required to accomplish it.

1. *Budget.* In either case, an annual budget must be prepared to guide the financial operations. The amount per pupil which this budget needs to provide will vary with many factors. If a salary item for employed workers is included, the average per pupil will of course be much higher than when this is not the case. The budget needs to be realistic in terms of the financial resources available, yet it must be ample to meet the requirements for good Christian education. Most churches spend far too little for this purpose, in light of its importance. At times it may be necessary to supplement regular income with special financial efforts to get the resources for larger expenditures.

The committee on Christian education has the responsibility for making and administering the budget. This committee will get a statement of financial needs from the agencies of the church school, work these into a unified budget, and recommend it to the financial committee of the church. Once the budget has been approved, each agency should strive to live within its allowances, though it should retain the privilege of adjusting items within the total budget as this may become desirable.

2. *What should be included?* The budget should include provision for all necessary expenditures. The largest item will probably be that for curriculum materials. Experience of previous years will usually be a guide to the

amount needed. To this there needs to be added an amount for rental and purchases of audio-visuals; teacher training, including registration fees at training schools, expenses of delegates to summer conferences, special speakers; supplies, such as paper, pencils, and crayons; books for the workers' library; new equipment; and a reasonable item for contingent expenses which cannot be anticipated at the time the budget is made.

When the offerings of pupils go toward the church budget, there is no need to include an item for missions in the Christian education budget. On the other hand, if the church school retains the offerings for its own support, provision needs to be made for some of the money to go to "others" so that pupils may learn missionary giving. If sufficient funds are available, it is appropriate also for a portion of the budget to be designated for the church.

3. *Expenditures.* The business procedures of the church school should be sound. It is wise to have one purchasing agent to whom requisitions will be referred, and who will approve bills for payment. Workers should understand that they have the right to make such requests, and do not need to use their own money for what they must buy. Those who must make frequent small purchases may be allowed a petty cash fund.

4. *Special Projects.* The financial policy here recommended assumes that the offerings from each agency go to the church treasury, and that each receives its support from the same source. This is valuable in teaching proper church support. It does not condone some groups having their own "kitties" to use as they please. Does this plan remove the causes for which people give too far from the interest and experience of the givers? This is not the case with that part of a pledge which goes to church support,

but there may be this effect with respect to missionary projects, which the pupils usually have no part in determining. The difficulty can be overcome in part through education in the purpose of the budget. But is there a place for special projects for classes, departments, or other groups? We regard such special causes as no violation of the principle advanced, as long as the pledge to the church is understood and maintained. There are several plans for a "youth budget" which would be of this type; also the "workday for Christ" participated in by many youth groups. Departments and classes may get interested in special causes to which they want to give.

5. *Education in Stewardship.* The need for financial support must not be too far separated from education in Christian giving. Pupils should never feel that they are only paying for what they get. Emphasize the reasons for giving more than the amount of the offering. Giving should be an expression of worship, and the offering should be included as an element in the worship service. This was dealt with in chapter 7, pages 119-120.

POSTSCRIPT

In the preceding pages, we have tried to present workable plans and programs for an effective church school. Some of these suggestions will not be new to our readers, for there are good workers and good church schools throughout our country. Others, if they are accepted, may require changes and innovations. We are well aware that it is easier to suggest changes than to bring them to pass. Church people, and especially the older members, are likely to be conservative and to like things as they are.

Do not expect to do the impossible, or to revolutionize things too fast. Education is a slow process. A little accomplished at a time will add up to a great deal in the course of a few years. Accept the limitations of your situation as far as you must, without undue frustration, but let your vision find ways of having better Christian education under the conditions which you must meet.

One of the qualifications of a good administrator is the ability to establish and maintain good public relations. Your job is education, and you must carry your people along with you in making changes if they are to be permanently effective. Unlimited patience and perseverance in persuading others of the rightness of what you so clearly see will accomplish more than knocking their heads together. In time they may come to accept your point of view, and may even get the idea that they thought of it first.

The committee on Christian education should be a great help in all this, for it provides an opportunity to convince a small and representative group, who in turn may be influential in convincing others. There is strength also in having the whole congregation accept its responsibility for Christian education, as it properly should, and confronting the members frequently with the work of the church school. Support your position with the authority usually accorded to books, audio-visuals, and prominent guest speakers. If they can win your battle for you, it does not matter who gets the glory, as long as the desired result is achieved.

Since our approach has been that of dealing with problems of the church school, we may have given the impression that the life of the church school leader consists only of problems and heartaches, of thorns and never a rose. This is not the case. It also has its glory and joy. The glory is that of working in the most important undertaking of the church, of serving him whom we call Master. The joy is that of working with a selected group of God's people in the church school staff, and with them, seeing generations of young people growing up in discipleship to that same Master.

15 PROBLEMS IN CHURCH SCHOOL LEADERSHIP

Here is a list of 250 problems relating to church school organization, administration, and supervision, with references to pages where answers may be found in this book.

Adults

Why is Christian education of adults important? (40)
How should adult classes be organized and taught? (40, 41, 65)
What is included in Christian education of adults? (40)
What is the nature and work of the home department? (186)

Audio-Visuals

What is the place of audio-visual aids in the curriculum? (94)
How may audio-visuals be most effectively used? (95, 96)
How may audio-visuals be used in parent-teacher meetings? (178, 179)

Awards and Other Recognition

What considerations should determine the policy with respect to awards? (146-149)

How should a system of recognition be administered? (149)
What kinds of reports to parents on pupil progress may be
used? (149, 150, 181)
Should Bibles and other gifts be given to pupils? How may the
giving of Bibles be financed? (150, 151)

Choirs

How may the work of choirs contribute to Christian education? (66, 67)

Church, The

What is the nature and purpose of the church? (9-11)
What are the functions of the church? (11-14)
How should the church be organized? (14-16)
How does the quality of Christian fellowship in the church
contribute to Christian education? (19-21)
How may the agencies of the church be kept in integral rela-
tion to the whole? (15)

Church School

Why does the church need a church school? (21)
What is included in the church school? (32)
What is the difference between the church school and the
Sunday school? (32)
How should the church school be organized by divisions, de-
partments, and classes? (34-36)
What are "agencies" of Christian education? How are they
related to the church school? (36, 37)
What adaptations in organization are recommended for small
churches? For large churches? (37, 38)
Should the church school have a constitution? (41-44)
What is a church school cabinet? (60, 61)
How may Boy Scouts and other clubs be related to the church
school? (66)

Christian Education

What is the meaning of Christian education? (16, 17)
What is the place of Christian education in the church? (16, 17)
What are the aims of Christian education? (17, 18)

What principles for Christian education follow from the nature and purpose of the church? (22, 23)

Classes

Should boys and girls be separated in church school classes? (38, 39)

How large should church school classes and other groups be? (39, 40)

Committee on Christian Education

What are the purpose and duties of a committee on Christian education? (27, 48-52)

How should members of this committee be chosen? (28)

Who should be chairman of the committee? (29)

How often should meetings be held? How should they be conducted? Who should prepare the agenda? (29, 30)

Is a committee on Christian education necessary in a small church? What adaptations are recommended? (29)

What is the pastor's relation to the committee on Christian education? (30, 31)

What is the superintendent's relation to the committee on Christian education? (31, 32)

How should this committee be organized? (29, 30)

How may a new committee be started, or an inactive committee re-vitalized? (32)

What is the committee's responsibility for enlistment and training of workers? (196)

What is the committee's responsibility for the budget of the church school? (262)

Constitution

Should the church school have a constitution? (41-44)

What is the value of a manual of procedure? (67)

Curriculum (See also **Lesson Materials**)

What is meant by curriculum? (69)

What kind of experiences contribute most to Christian growth? (69-73)

How is evangelism related to curriculum? (72)

What is the relation between curriculum and published lesson materials? (73)
How do curriculum materials differ in underlying presuppositions and content? (79-81)

Director of Christian Education

What is the work of a director of Christian education? (55, 56)
What is the pastor's responsibility for Christian education when there is a director? (56)

Discipline

What is the meaning of discipline? (152, 153)
What constitutes good order? (153-155)
What type of discipline is best? (154, 155)
Why do pupils misbehave? (156-159)
In what sense are teachers also under discipline? (155, 158)
How may good order be secured and maintained? (159-165)

Divisions and Departments

How should the church school be organized by divisions and departments? (34, 35)
What adaptations are desirable for small churches? Large churches? (37, 38)
What is the purpose and value of having a superintendent for each of the divisions of the church school? How are they related to the general superintendent? (61)
What are the duties of principals of departments? (61-63)
What other officers do departments need? (63)

Equipment (See Rooms and Equipment)

Finances

How should the church school be financed? (261, 262)
Who should make the budget? (262)
What should be included in the budget? (262, 263)
Should groups in the church be allowed to keep their offerings for their own purposes? (263)
Should special service projects be encouraged, apart from the regular budget? (264)

What is the primary purpose of the church school offering?
(264)

Home and Church School

To what extent is Christian education dependent on the
home? (168)
How should the work of teachers be related to the home? (169)
What may parents expect of the church school? (170, 171)
What has a church school teacher a right to expect of the
home? (171, 172)
How can we cultivate interest on the part of the home? (172-187)
Why should teachers visit the homes of pupils? (174-176)
Why is it difficult to get teachers to visit homes? (175, 176)
How may teachers be helped in making home visits? (176)
How may parent-teacher meetings be made effective? (177-181)
How may family worship services and special days be used to
enhance home cooperation? (109, 181)
What part should parents take in the work of the church
school? (182-185)
What are class sponsors, and how may they be used? (184)
How may the church school be made a cooperative venture of
the parents? (184, 185)

Home Department

What is the purpose of the home department? (65, 66)
How should the home department be conducted? (186)
Where do we get literature for study by home department
members? (186)

Home Work

What kind of out-of-class work is desirable? For what ages?
(141, 142)
Why are home assignments necessary? (143)
What may be done by teachers to get pupils to accept and do
home work? (143-145)

Lesson Materials

What is the purpose of published lesson materials? (74, 75)
What types of lesson materials are available? What are the

respective merits of each type? (75-79)

Who should choose the lesson materials? (83)

What kind of studies are necessary before adopting lesson materials? (82-86)

By what criteria should lesson materials be judged and chosen? (86-88)

Should a single series of lessons be used, or selections be made from different sources? (88, 89)

Should individual teachers ever be allowed to choose their own materials? (89)

Should a church always use the publications of its own denomination? (89, 90)

Where should a union church school get its curriculum materials? (90, 91)

What steps may be taken to assure effective use of lesson materials? (91, 92)

How should the handling of lesson materials be administered? (93, 94)

Leadership (See Workers)

Library

What is the value in having a church library? (66)

What kind of materials should the church library provide? (66)

How may the library best be used in helping workers? (219, 220)

Missions

Why should missionary education be part of the curriculum? (97)

How may missionary education be made most effective? (97)

Where may resources for missionary education be found? (97)

Nursery Roll

What is the purpose of the nursery roll? (65, 66)

How should the nursery roll be administered? (186)

Objectives

What is the objective of Christian education? (17, 18, 83, 84)

How are objectives related to curriculum? (83, 84)

How and by whom should the objectives of Christian education in a local church be determined? (83, 84)

What are the objectives for the training of workers? (211, 212)

Officers

What kind of leadership is most effective? (45)

What general officers should the church school have? (52-61)

What departmental officers are needed? (61-63)

How should officers be elected? (49)

Organization

What is the relation between organization and program? (24)

How should the church be organized for Christian education? (25-27)

How should the church school be organized? (34, 35)

Pastor

What is the pastor's relation to the committee on Christian education? (30, 31)

What is the pastor's place and work in Christian education? (52-55)

Why not leave the church school to lay workers and free the pastor for other duties? (55)

Pupils

How does the nature of the pupils affect aim and method? (18)

How should pupils be graded? (34, 36)

How can the interest and attendance of young people be held? (257, 258)

What is the church's responsibility for out-reach to those not in church school? (260)

What are some practical plans for increasing enrollment? (260, 261)

Records

What is the purpose of keeping church school records? (249)

What should be included in the church school records? (249, 251)

What is the value of a unified system of records for the whole church school? (250, 251)

What meaning should be given to such terms as enrollment, attending membership, attendance, etc.? (251)

When should a pupil be enrolled? (252)

When should a pupil be withdrawn or put on an inactive list? (252, 253)

What constitutes a good percentage of attendance? (254)

How should records be administered and used? (254, 255)

✗ How may the problem of post-confirmation attendance be handled? (257, 258)

Rooms and Equipment

How is program affected by rooms and equipment? (236)

What kind of studies need to precede the planning of a new building? (238-240)

What principles should guide in planning a new building? (238)

How can a one-room church meet the problem of rooms and equipment? (242, 243)

How can a large room be divided for classes? (244)

What kind of equipment is desirable for worship rooms? Classrooms? (245, 246)

Why is servicing of rooms and equipment important? (247, 248)

How may an old building be made more useful through remodeling? (247, 248)

How may workers be trained in proper use of equipment? (248)

Secretary

What are the duties of the church school secretary? (59, 60)

Special Days and Seasons

What is the value of observing special days and seasons? (99)

Why should this be considered a part of curriculum? (99)

How may special days and seasons be made effective for Christian education? (99, 100)

What special days should be observed? (100-104)

What should be the nature of children's day observances? (102, 103)

Where can we get program material for children's day? (103)

Should national holidays be observed in the church school? (103, 104)

Stewardship

What is the place of stewardship in Christian education? (98, 261)

How should education in Christian stewardship be given? (98, 99)

Should pupils give to the budget of the church, toward the expenses of the church school, or to special causes? (98, 99)

What is the chief purpose of the church school offering? (264)

Superintendent

What is the relation of the superintendent of the church school to the committee on Christian education? (31, 32)

Should the general superintendent be responsible for the whole church school, or only for the Sunday school? (56)

What should be the qualifications of a church school superintendent? (56, 57)

What are the duties of the superintendent? (57-59)

Should the superintendent be a man, or may a woman serve in this position? (57)

How long should the superintendent hold office? (59)

Should the church school have an assistant superintendent? If so, what duties may be assigned to him? (59)

What is the relation of the general superintendent to the division superintendents and department principals? (61, 62)

Should the general superintendent act as supervisor of teaching? (218, 219)

Tardiness

How may the problem of tardiness be met? (258, 259)

Teachers (See also Workers; Training)

What are the duties of church school teachers? (64)

What conditions must be met by teachers if their work is to be effective? (133-137)

How may a teacher best get acquainted with his pupils? (134, 135)

What values are there in visiting homes? (135)

What standards should be set for teachers? (137-141)

Time Schedules

What should be the length of church school sessions? of class sessions? (259, 260)

How will good administration help in preserving the maximum time? (260)

Training

What are the conditions for a successful training program? (210, 211)

What are the objectives for the training of workers? (211, 212)

What is pre-service training? How may it be provided? (213, 214)

What is the best way to start a new teacher in his work? (214)

What are some do's and don'ts for a new teacher? (215-218)

What is the place and importance of personal guidance in training workers? (218, 219)

How may the church library serve as a resource for teachers? (219, 220)

How may observation and demonstration be used in training? (220)

How may new teachers learn through guided practice? (220, 221)

What is the nature and value of a workshop in the training of workers? (221)

How may group conferences be used? (221)

What is the nature and value of a workers' retreat? (229, 230)

What types of training classes for workers are available, and how may they best be used? (230-233)

How can we motivate our workers to accept and participate in training? (234, 235)

Treasurer

What are the duties of the church school treasurer? How is he related to the treasurer of the church? (60)

Vacation Church School

How should the vacation church school be organized? (64, 65)

How is it related to the committee on Christian education? (64, 65)

How should attendance at the vacation church school be promoted? (261)

Weekday Church School

How is the weekday church school related to the total educational program of the church? (65)

Workers

Why is the problem of leadership the No. 1 problem in most churches? (189, 190)

Are professional workers the answer to this problem? (190, 191)

Should the pastor be expected to give professional leadership to the church school? (192)

Why must lay workers do most of the Christian education in Protestant churches? (192-194)

What factors exist in most churches which make the enlistment of workers difficult? What is the remedy? (194)

What is the nature and purpose of a parish life conference? (194, 195)

Where may prospective workers be found? (196)

What qualifications should be expected of church school workers? (196-198)

Are men or women to be preferred as teachers? (197, 198)

Should high school boys and girls be used as teachers? (198)

What motivations may be used in enlisting workers? (198, 199)

How long should a teacher or officer hold his position? (199, 200)

Are leaves of absence for faithful workers desirable? (201)

How should prospective workers be enlisted? (200-204)

How soon may new members of the church be approached for service? (200)

How should new workers be started in their work? (204-207)

What is a commissioning service for workers? What kind of program is recommended? (206)

How can we get rid of ineffective workers? (207, 208)

What should be our policy with respect to substitute teachers? (208, 209)

Workers' Conference

What is the workers' conference? (222)

What purposes does it serve? (222)

What is good policy with respect to meetings of the workers' conference? (223, 224)

What should be the nature of the program? (224-229)

What are some suggested program topics? (226, 227)

What should be the time schedule for the workers' conference meeting? (227, 228)

How may attendance be promoted? (228)

How should the meeting room be arranged for best results? (228)

Worship

Why should worship be considered a part of the curriculum of Christian education? (105, 106)

What is the nature and purpose of the service of worship? (106, 107)

Should church school pupils participate in the general church service? (108)

What are some practical plans for relating children to church worship? (108-110)

What are the values in church school department worship? (110, 111)

How should pupils be grouped for worship? (111, 112)

Should there be an assembly for worship for the whole school? (112)

How can we have graded worship in a church with just one room? (111, 112)

Should the departmental service of worship precede or follow classes? (112, 113)

If the service precedes classes, should there be an additional period of closing worship? (112, 113)

What type of worship service is recommended for each of the departments? (113, 114)

What are the qualities of a good worship service? (113)

Who should lead worship? Should pupils have a part in leadership? (116-118)

What is an order of worship? What elements should be included? (118)

What are examples of suitable orders of worship? (120-125)

Where do we get help in planning worship? (125, 126)

Where should departmental services of worship be conducted? May the church sanctuary be used? (126, 127)

Is a chapel for children recommended? (126)

How may pupils be taught the meaning and practice of worship? (127-129)

How can we get pupils to join in singing? (128)

How should leaders of worship be trained? (129-132)